SAIL THE CINQUE PORTS

Rod

with every good wish

Robert

Robert Crane

Sail the Cinque Ports © Robert Crane 2005

Robert Crane asserts the moral right to be identified as the
Author of this Work.

Chart extracts reproduced by permission of the
Controller of Her Majesty's Stationery Office and
The U.K. Hydrographic Office
www.ukho.gov.uk
© Crown Copyright

Town maps reproduced by permission of Estate Publications
© Estate Publications
Crown Copyright reserved: Licence No 100019031

ISBN 0-9551116-0-9

Printed by
Ashford Overload Services Ltd.
Bottings Industrial Estate, Hillsons Road, Curdridge, Southampton
SO30 2DY
01489 787621

Published by
Robert Crane
Market Walls, Chichester, West Sussex
PO19 1JU
01243 527308

Front Cover: Sandwich Town Quay
Back Cover: The Author's 'Jemima Puddleduck'

SAIL THE CINQUE PORTS

A Short History

with

Town Guides, Gazetteers,

Chartlets and Sailing Itinerary

Robert Crane

INTRODUCTION

THE PASSAGE from Chichester along the Sussex and Kent coasts is a reminder of the Cinque Ports - always pronounced in the anglicised *'sink'* – that for centuries were the most important in the country. Under Hastings, Romney, Hythe, Dover and Sandwich there were nearly thirty other ports, harbours, towns or villages as Members or 'Limbs' within an administration that extended from east Sussex into Essex, and their role was pivotal in the creation of a Nation out of medieval England.

They were much affected by the coastal changes that resulted in some being distanced from navigable waters. Even with my Peter Duck shoal-draft motor-sailer on her way home from the east coast, I could enter only a half-dozen of the thirty; they were enough to draw me into a series of fascinating experiences, thoroughly good sailing, and the magical satisfaction of making new landfalls.

Numerous distinguished historians and writers have shared that fascination; their works are legion, but there has been little further since the 1970's. This contribution would have made poor progress without the enthusiastic encouragement of harbour masters, librarians and town councils, to say nothing of family and friends.

My descriptions follow the convention of a counter-clockwise order around the coast. They are restricted to those with sailing potential, and they would have done gross injustice had I not familiarised myself with their historical background. There are others of more limited navigability and lesser interest that I have reduced to a short section.

I add the customary cautions that no responsibility is accepted for inaccuracies and, for the mariner, that this book is no substitute for up-to-date charts and pilotage information. The gazetteer contents were checked this year, but they are necessarily prone to change; the inclusion of an establishment or service is not to be taken as a recommendation, and neither do I apologise for idiosyncrasies in selection.

I hope that this book will encourage readers to share my voyage of exploration.

Robert Crane
Chichester, August 2005

CONTENTS

A HISTORY of the CINQUE PORTS

THE CINQUE PORTS of east Sussex and Kent were, at one time, the most important in the country, long before the ports of London, Southampton, Bristol and Liverpool were of any significance. Today, Hastings has no harbour other than its shingle beach for the fishing fleet, New Romney is nearly a couple of miles inland, Hythe has no haven, Dover alone is castle and port as it has always been, and Sandwich barely retains a town quay of sorts.

Their medieval ascendancy provides one of the most fascinating epochs in the emergence of England's nation state; at the height of their importance, they were responsible for the administration of some two-dozen other harbours, towns and villages, and their admiralty jurisdiction extended from off Seaford in Sussex to Galloper Beacon and The Naze in Essex. Their subsequent decline, due largely to their natural limitations, was against a background of breathtaking arrogance, smuggling and piracy that continued into the late nineteenth century.

At the end of the eighth century, the regional topography combined the vastly forested Downs with coastal cliffs to the east, plains and marshlands to the north, and low-lying woodlands and marshlands to the south; the island of Thanet was then defined by the Wantsum Channel which provided a generous anchorage and a safe passage avoiding the North Foreland. This region had few communications by land, it was therefore the most independent and, as the nearest to mainland Europe, it was targeted by raiders and settlers alike. The Romans established their fortress and supply base at Richborough, just off the Wantsum; with their withdrawal, it was from this region that the northern European immigrants displaced the native Celts, and it was their pugnacious territorial aggression that was later harnessed as a coastal defensive force. Hastings then had its harbour, New Romney and Hythe were at the head of an extensive shallow sea, Dover had already commenced its battle against silting, and Sandwich was on the west bank of the Wantsum.

The ports were small fishing and trading communities whose natives relied on an intimate knowledge of the local waters; the Bronze Age craft at Dover Museum is the earliest excavated sea-going vessel in the world, similar to a fifty-foot paddled punt ideal for the creeks and estuaries, and used also for cross-channel trading in fair weather. In contrast, the immigrant Norse were great explorers whose exploits extended from the eastern Mediterranean to north America, by following the stars and bird migrations; their early longships were superb sea boats, either as the *sneccars* principally oared for fighting, or as the later and more commodidious *knorrs* which were sailed for migrating; with few modifications, their design was used for more than a thousand years, and as depicted on the Bayeux Tapestry.

The average sized longboat had between fifteen and twenty pairs of oars, but the largest known was that of King Olaf Trygesson at 165ft overall, with a displacement of 250 tons and a full complement of 400 men; the Saxon Chronicles describe a Danish raiding party of two hundred and fifty ships up the old course of the River Rother, that could have landed over a thousand men with their camp-followers, and would have been most difficult to displace.

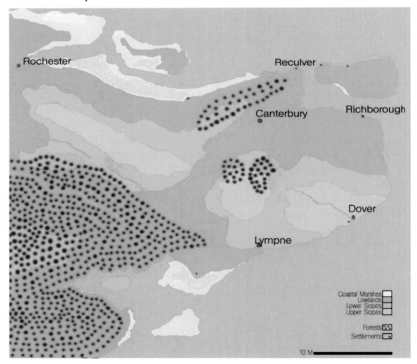

The Early Topography of East Kent

The ninth century saw the enormous plundering raids by the Danes. King Alfred's strong fleet manned by mercenaries kept them in check, and a hundred years later it was King Edgar's even larger fleet that secured stability. The only facilities available for building and victualling in the southeast would have been at the five major ports, and perhaps a few smaller ones; these had many shared experiences in their fisheries, trade and defence, but there is no record of any early cooperation among them .

One of the earliest feudal grants was that of King Canute in 1031, when he '... *gave to Christ's church in Canterbury the haven of Sandwich, and all rights that arise therefrom, on either side of the haven; so that when the tide is highest and fullest, and there be a man standing on the ship with a taper-axe in hand, whithersoever the large taper-axe might be thrown out of the ship, throughout all that land the ministers of Christ's Church should enjoy their rights ...'*. The recorded annual rent of fifty pounds and forty thousand herrings discloses something of the regional wealth.

This *ad hoc* state of affairs extended to sea-borne defence. In about 1050, Edward the Confessor addressed this by replacing the mercenary system with ship service; under this, every coastal town was required to provide ships and men at times of hostilities, a practice long adopted by the northern European tribes in the form of a *levy* of ships of designated sizes. Edward, in applying this in England, granted the chartered towns a considerable degree of self-government in recognition of their duty.

This applied to the five southern ports and, from the date of their simultaneous charters, they were customarily referred to as the Cinque Ports. Unique to them however, was the extent of their rights and relief from taxes, and their obligation to provide a standing force; one of the most interesting and unrecorded contemporary aspects was the acknowledgement of their own Court of Shepway, an institution assumed to have arisen from the necessity of their dealing directly with the crown.

Initially, their shared service comprised the provision of fifty-seven ships and men for fifteen days a year at the towns' expense and thereafter at the crown's, but always at twenty-one days' notice of call. The provision of ships for both defence and for the transport of the royal retinue was allocated among the ports, and the notice was required to recall them from fishing expeditions; the fifteen days' service reflected the time usually needed to repel Danish raids, and corresponded to that allowed for a weather-dependent channel crossing and return.

These feudal grants were, in reality, only an acknowledgement of the Ports' growing and almost uncontrollable influence. In 1051, the high-handed Count Eustace of Normandy, whilst a guest of the king, caused a serious affray with the people of Dover; the earl Godwin declined the king's orders to punish the town without fair trial, and was banished to Flanders. He returned in 1052 to regain contact with the king's son, Harold, and they collected a fleet from Pevensey, Romney, Hythe and Folkestone; the king's fleet avoided a confrontation and retreated to London; there was a principle at stake, and civil war was narrowly avoided.

The shipbuilding of the day took place on the beaches nearest the forests, with little organisation. The battle tactics were similarly rough and ready, with reliance on short bursts of speed to ram the opponent and to continue with hand to hand fighting; the Portsmen relied on their intimate knowledge of the tides and shallows, and probably removed some of the frames from the boats to increase manoeuvrability; it was left to each boat to select its opponent, and there was no more teamwork than would be found in a swarm of hornets. The fore and aft castles added for both conning and fighting initially were awkward demountables, and it was only a little before the Norman invasion that they became permanent platforms for the archers.

The Bayeux tapestry depicts the ships as mostly without castles; the advantages of a high freeboard for fighting were already well known by the Viking domestic fleets, but were not much adopted in the English waters for another hundred years. It is clear also from the tapestry that sail power was already of significance for transport, but nevertheless oared propulsion was to remain common for a long time.

The ship service expanded beyond the channel; in 1063 they supported the campaign against the Welsh and in 1066 they were engaged in the North Sea repelling the Norse. King Harold's short reign was contested by William of Normandy, and was disturbed by his half-brother Tostig from Norway who had attacked Sandwich; this coincided with protracted hostilities with the Dutch, and it is doubtful if the Conquest would have succeeded had the Portsmen been in their home waters. The invasion met with strong resistance, and many of the conquered Ports received heavy treatment; Hastings was burned, Romney suffered revenge for mauling one of the invasion fleets, Dover town too was burned and the troops committed savage rape and plunder.

William, as an able politician, secured support to repulse the Danish raids that continued until the Ports inflicted heavy losses on an invading fleet off Sandwich in 1069. He recognised their importance in defence and communications by the renewal of their charters; this was later rewarded by the fleets' support for the Scottish expedition of King William II in 1091, when the loss of the large part of it had a disastrous effect on their small communities.

The 1086 Domesday Book provided the monarch with a working knowledge of his conquered territory. The population of Kent was then in the region of 45,000, and the recorded manorial rights were extensive; they included those to hold court, to run gaols as a source of profit, to treasure trove, and to a share in wrecks which would otherwise have been crown property. The Ports were recorded as possessing many privileges, although often subject to ecclesiastical rights; for Romney, ' ... *but the king has all service due from them, and they themselves have all other dues and fines, in return for the service upon the sea*' ; for Hythe, '... *and there belonged ... 21 burgesses of whom the king has sea service, and therefore they are quit ...* [of tolls]'; for Sandwich, '*... and pays the king sea service like Dover'.* Dover was referred to as a Royal Borough which acknowledged no over-lord but the King, and its status ranked alongside that of its Cinque Port charter; it was exempted from taxes in return for which '*the burgesses supplied the king once in the year 20 ships for 15 days, and in each ship were 21 men. This ... they did because he had remitted to them the sac and soc'*, 'sac and soc' being the sort of business with which a local court was competent to deal; the burgesses also provided a ferry service for the King's Messenger, at a fixed but a modest tariff.

It was from this time too, that the Ports' reliance on fishing and local trading expanded into substantial commerce. Sandwich became the leading port in the country for trade whilst London was still in its infancy; Dover became the leading port for passage to the continent, and was also given the right to establish money-changing facilities for the benefit of both tradesmen and the numerous pilgrims in both directions. England's coastal fisheries had greatly expanded in response to a growing population, and were of international importance, but it was Yarmouth that had already achieved the substantial combination of fishing and trading.

The importance of the North Sea herring fisheries cannot be overstated. The stocks were vast and, although their uncertain patterns of shoaling led to localised gluts and shortages, it was a stock upon which the fishing fleets of the day had little impact. The passage from the Sussex ports to the North Sea was a lengthy one and, in the absence of storage techniques, their rights from time immemorial at Yarmouth were vital; the principal rights were of *den and strond,* allowing them to land their catches and dry their nets on the beach. Yarmouth's annual fair lasted forty days to coincide with the autumnal herring catches, and it attracted over 1,000 vessels from home and abroad. The town looked to its increased status, and its demands for increased control over the fair resulted in even deeper conflicts with the Ports, and these were to continue for centuries.

The Ports' growing strength encouraged their piratical activities, and their cross-channel raids on the French ports were only nominally defensive; there were blurred distinctions between pre-emptive strikes and outright piracy. The primary function of the Shepway was to allocate ship service, but it also heard claims for the distribution of spoils; there were many complaints against the Portsmen, and the Crown was later required to compensate foreign merchants who had been attacked. In these raids, neither side spared the churches, because these were the strongest buildings and used for the storage of valuables; their bells were used as warning signals of impending attacks, and their seizure therefore was no mere trophy-hunting.

Kent was peaceful and prosperous in the late eleventh century, with substantial agricultural exports. It followed in the next century that the channel was no more than an inconvenient ditch between Anglo-Norman communities sharing the same crown; there was little need for large assemblies of ships of war, but they continued to be required as a royal ferry service and to repel piratical raiders. Their ships played a major part in the crusading fleet that captured Lisbon from the Moors in 1147, and again in 1190 when they provided about thirty of the fleet of a hundred ships which carried King Richard I's crusaders.

The importance of the services was such that the original Ports were unable to cope with the demand at a time of economic expansion, and numerous others joined as Members or 'Limbs'. Almost the whole of Kent's coastline, extending into Sussex and Essex, came under their control; at the peak of their influence, over thirty harbours and villages were involved. The Members were subject to supervision of their town management, and contributed to the Head Port's ship service; in return they received some of the privileges and, more importantly, support in dealing with the feudal overlords until such times as they were chartered in their own right.

There were various processes of attachment, and the informality of the Confederation of the Cinque Ports is emphasised by the dates often being unrecorded. In some cases, the reason for the association between Head Port and Member was merely the result of increasing commercial contact; in some, it was merely an *ad hoc* arrangement; for some, it was an avoidance of feudal impositions, and for others it was imposed by royal grant to assist the Head Port with the revenues.

The new charters extended their privileges even further. They were freed of '*lastage, tallage, pasage, kayage, rivage, ponsage, and wreck and other tolls and customs*'; they were entitled to trade '*lovescope-free*', unhindered by any monopoly or merchant guild. Their unique rights were reaffirmed, being those to their own courts, to the '*den and strond*' at Yarmouth and to the 'Coronation Honours' at Court. The Coronation Honours entitled them to carry the future monarch's canopy in the coronation procession, and to be seated at the monarch's table at the coronation banquet; this was yet another frictional assertion of their status which elevated them above that of the ecclesiastical aristocracy. The first recorded occasion at which this was exercised was that of King Richard I in 1189, but it is thought to have much earlier origins, and it is one which has continued to the present day, albeit with modification.

There was also the need for a greater degree of local government and accordingly there were numerous charters dating from this period, including those to the smaller ports of Kent; the charters hence elevated those towns to the status of Cinque Ports in their own right. Rye and

Winchelsea had long since been granted to the Monastery of Fifchamp in Normandy, and were members of Hastings; with the rise in hostilities with France, King Henry III took direct control of them *'for the better defence of the realm'*. With his award of charters to these two towns, the title of the Confederation became 'The Cinque Ports and the Two Antient Towns'.

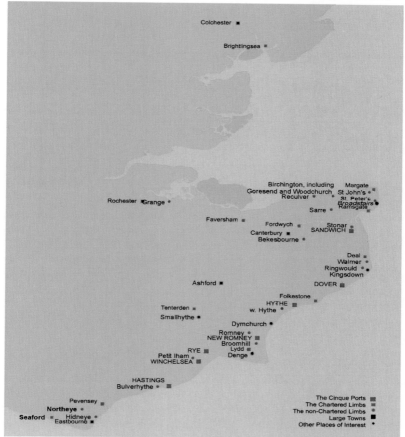

Colchester ■

Brightlingsea ■

Rochester ■Grange •

Birchington, including   Margate
Goresend and Woodchurch St John's •
            Reculver •   Broadstairs •
                    Sarre • Ramsgate

Faversham ■

Fordwych ■   Stonar ■
Canterbury ■   SANDWICH ■
Bekesbourne •

Deal ■
Walmer •
Ringwould • •
Kingsdown

Ashford ■

DOVER ■

Folkestone •
HYTHE ■
Tenterden ■   w. Hythe •
Smallhythe •

Dymchurch •

Romney •
NEW ROMNEY ■
Broomhill •
RYE ■   Lydd ■
Petit Iham •   Denge •
WINCHELSEA ■

HASTINGS
Bulverhythe • ■

Pevensey ■
Northeye •
Seaford ■ Hidneye •
    Eastbourne ■

The Cinque Ports ■
The Chartered Limbs ■
The non-Chartered Limbs •
Large Towns ■
Other Places of Interest •

The Cinque Ports and [from time to time] their Members

The growing status of the Shepway had attracted the attention of King Henry II. In 1228 he decreed that the Court of Pleas of the Cinque Ports should be held at Shepway every August *'which is an idle time for the men of those parts, as they have returned from various regions whither they had gone with their merchandise, and are awaiting the harvest time, and the time of fishing on the coast of England'*. The court's almost unfettered jurisdiction left the barons answerable to the King alone, and excused them from attendance at the shire court at Penenden Heath; their status undoubtedly caused anger because Yarmouth and Donwich in Suffolk being in contention with the Ports, also were required to attend the Shepway. The court became one of record, and was empowered to hear offences of treason and murder, and well as of felony and lesser offences, and those of wreck. Whilst the death sentence of the Shepway was executed by hanging, there grew one custom peculiarly appropriate to the local courts of the Ports in that execution was by drowning; known locations for this include the Aston stream at Bulverhythe near Hastings, and the Delf stream at Sandwich.

The court was composed of the towns' officers, together with townsmen called for the purpose of selecting a jury; it continued to meet in the open, but there were the major shortcomings of irregularity and the requirement for forty days' notice of attendance. The early recognition was an expedient service to a collection of communities who had common interests, and whose folk were often on relatively distant expeditions; as with every occasion of recognition granted to the Ports it became a jealously guarded privilege which was near insufferable to those 'in the foreign', or otherwise residing beyond the privilege. The growing status of the court required a more formal acknowledgement of the royal presiding officer and it was confirmed as that of Lord Warden who, in recognisance, was required to affirm allegiance to the Ports on taking office; the commencement of this constitutionally unique office was probably as an *ad hoc* arrangement, as the first formal appointment was in the reign of King John. The defences for the south-east were, at that time, split between the sea and land-based forces with the fundamental weakness of separate commands; it would be another hundred years before the command was integrated under the office of the Constable of Dover Castle with its admiralty jurisdiction.

In the second half of the twelfth century King Henry II confirmed the right of the Hastings Barons to hold their own court at the Yarmouth fair, as well as the rights to '*den and strond*'; this caused even more resentment, and particularly so of the well-intentioned duty imposed on the Portsmen to provide their own bailiffs. There were numerous confrontations which ended with the loss of ships and lives; in one instance, a Cinque Ports' bailiff was killed by one of Yarmouth; on another, when a chapel was built for the benefit of visiting sailors and a Yarmouth priest was appointed, the Portsmen threw him out and appointed one of their own.

When King John had ascended the throne in 1199, England's sea power was unchallenged. There was some justification for the proclamation of the 'sovereignty of the sea' made at Hastings Castle in March 1201: '*That if the Lieutenant of the King ... in any voyage appointed ... do at sea meet with any shyps or vessels empty or laden which will not stryke and vail their bonnets at the command of the King's Lieutenant ...*' he was empowered to treat them effectively as enemies. This was not as imperious as it might seem, because much of the naval effort was in the protection of English merchantmen; the Cinque Ports naturally took it upon themselves to claim equivalent recognition, including that from the fleets of other English ports; Winchelsea was here the most aggressive, but it was refuted by the men of Fowey, and led to a long-running battle between the two until Winchelsea was soundly trounced.

The thirteenth century was notable for its violence and for John's loss of Normandy; the channel became England's first line of defence, and the service of the Ports became so essential that he was unable to control their behaviour. In 1205, he granted them new charters to remind them of their defensive role; three years later, he ordered home their fleets to join up with his own, and also to provide experienced sailors in preparation for war. In 1213, they were instrumental in a pre-emptive strike against Dieppe, where they destroyed the town and attacked the assembly of French ships in the Seine, thus delaying invasion preparations. In the same year, the English fleet included a contingent of fifty ships from the Ports and, under Admiral William de Longspee, defeated the French in the Battle of Damme; there, the French lost hundreds of ships including many which were captured but, within two years, a French invasion appeared inevitable. John had to face commercial, as well as territorial, competition. The Hanseatic League, promoting trade among German cities, brought about a rapid increase in coastal trade that quickly extended to more distant waters. England's preoccupation both with domestic problems and with France was to have severe repercussions, leading to the signing of the Magna Carta and to her being left behind in maritime development; indeed, it was John's mismanagement which led to the Archbishop of Canterbury seeking the armed support of Louis of France.

In 1216, the coronation of King Henry III and his wife Eleanor was a magnificent affair; Matthew Paris, the monk-historian at St. Albans, recorded that *'the Barons ... carried over the King ... the silken cloth four-square, purple, supported by four silvered spears with four little silver-gilt bells, four Barons being assigned to every spear, lest Port should seem to be preferred to Port. Likewise the same bore a silken cloth over the Queen coming after the King, which said clothe they claim as theirs of right, and they obtained them at Court'.*

In the same year, the long-awaited French invasion almost led to an English collapse; the Isle of Wight was overrun, Dover town was razed, and Dover Castle was under siege notwithstanding the harrying of the French supply fleet. In 1217, under Hubert de Burgh as Lord Warden and Admiral of the Ports, some forty ships counter-attacked and sank or disabled eighty of the French, and the siege lifted. Again, in the following year, the much larger reinforcing French fleet was defeated decisively in the

Battle of Sandwich, thus removing the threat of a further invasion for many years. This was the first recorded occasion in which the fleet of the Ports acted in unison, instead of individually selecting and engaging their opponents; the remainder of the century saw the behaviour of the Ports at its worst, with numerous acts of piracy and riotous confrontations with Yarmouth, which the crown was unable to contain.

In 1267, Sir Roger de Leybourne was appointed to his second term as Lord Warden, and from then the office was combined with that of Constable of Dover Castle; his jurisdiction extended from Redciff in Sussex to Shoe Beacon in Essex, and outwards to mid-channel, or 'half-sea over'. Inherent to this was the establishment of an Admiralty Court at Dover, and its many functions included action against individuals or organisations that interfered with the Ports' navigation. Initially, the Court was held on the beach but it was soon removed to the castle; this was contrary to the Royal Grant by which the Portsmen were not required to 'plead in the foreign', and the court was removed to St. James Church in the fourteenth century.

The powers of the Admiralty and Borough courts came to overshadow the Shepway's importance; its use became limited to swearing in a new Lord Warden, to occasional trials of treason, counterfeiting and treasure trove, and to a court of appeal for the barons. The rivalry among the Ports precluded their submission to the jurisdiction of any town in matters affecting them as a whole; they had held informal meetings at the village of Broadhill on Romney Marsh since the thirteenth century, and accordingly they established the additional court of Brodhull which was functional as such by the late fifteenth century; the seemingly insignificant location near New Romney was chosen as being outside 'the jurisdiction of any of the Ports, but the village has long since disappeared. The minutes of their meetings have been preserved, and are known as the Black and White Books.

King Edward I commenced his campaigns against Wales in 1277, and his plans envisaged the isolation of Gwynned from its vital agricultural supplies in Anglesea, together with the construction of coastal fortifications. The protection of his seaward flank and an assurance of supplies were critical to his success; here the Cinque Ports gave their service as the major part of a fleet of twenty-seven of the largest vessels, together with their tenders and 608 sailors, all under the command of Stephen of Pencester, the then Lord Warden. The further uprising in 1282 was again decided by the strength of Edward's sea-power, with forty ships from London and the Cinque Ports; these included two galleys sent by Romney and Winchelsea, each with a crew of fifty instead of the usual complement of twenty. In recognition of this service, Edward granted the first of the great charters codifying the Ports' privileges, and setting out the allocation of their ship service. The grant to a Confederation, instead of to the individual Ports, did much to strengthen its status; under this, they were confirmed as quit of numerous crown taxes and were granted the valuable rights of *infangtheff and utgangtheff* [to judge thieves taken both inside and outside the Ports] and of wreck, together with their other privileges.

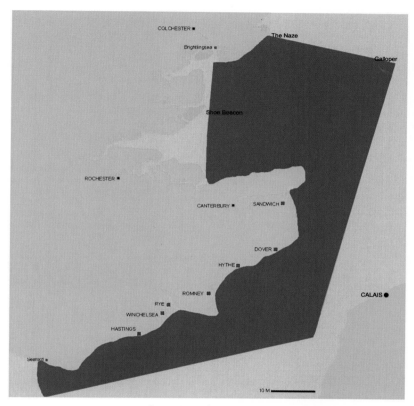

The Admiralty Jurisdiction of the Cinque Ports

Edward's expenditure forced him to instigate customs duties; the result was rampant smuggling by murderous bands of cutthroats who easily outmanoeuvred the ill-equipped revenue officers. The Ports had scant regard for the conventions of the day, were frequently at odds with the monastic estates, and quickly reverted to outright piracy; in 1290, they attacked and killed many of the Jews who had sought refuge from continental persecution; in 1292, in combination with fleets from the Dutch, Irish and Gascons, they fought the combined fleets of the Normans, French and Genoese in a private battle in the channel; they also continued their private wars with Fowey and with Bayonne. It was hardly surprising that they became known as the king's pirates, but their defensive importance was such that they escaped with no more than a royal reprimand. In the following year however, one hundred of the Ports' ships beat a French navy of twice the size, so successfully that the French were for a long time left short of both ships and men.

The series of natural disasters in the thirteenth century greatly reduced the ability of the Ports to respond to their sea service; the storm in October 1251 that destroyed over 300 houses and several churches on the south coast was but a foretaste. In 1252 a storm burst the shingle banks at Old Winchelsea and caused extensive damage to property and shipping; in 1253, a further storm deposited so much salt that the crops were poor in the following year; in 1284 the sea destroyed the village of Promhill, and the River Rother filled up at the mouth and made a new and shorter course through Rye, leaving high and dry the haven of Romney; Sandwich was reprieved temporarily, in that the Wantsum channel remained open on the south and west sides of Thanet. In 1287 there was the catastrophic storm that affected much of the southeast, and left untenable the Camber Sands on which Old Winchelsea was built; its abandonment was costly, but it was rebuilt on the hill at Iham and occupied from 1292. The severe storms continued into the early fourteenth century, only to be followed by a prolonged drought in the 1320's and a pestilence that affected the cattle.

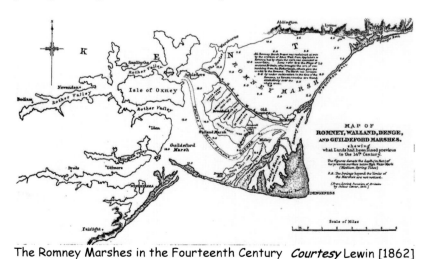

The Romney Marshes in the Fourteenth Century *Courtesy* Lewin [1862]

The continuing drift of shingle along the coast was having its effect, too. The port of New Romney had been silting up in the 1230's; by 1250 a great shingle bar built up at the entrance to Hythe; the port of Hastings was ever less serviceable, at Sandwich the River Wantsum and the harbour were being further encroached by sand banks, and Dover alone was

From Edward Knocker in "An Account of the Grand Court of Shepway" [1862]		From the Records drawn up by the Constable of Dover Castle [1293]		From the earlier Custumal of the Town of Hythe
		Hastings	3	Hastings shall find 21 ships, in each 21 men and a Boy [which is called a Gromet]. To it pertain, as the members of one Town, the sea shore in Seaford, Pevensey, Hordeneye, Winchelsea, Rye, Iham, Beckesbourne, Grenge, Northil, Bulverhythe.
Hastings,	Ships, 3	Lowey of Pevensey	1	
Pevensey,	1	Bulverhythe and		
Bulverhithe		and Petit-John	1	
& Petit Hiam	1	Grench at Gillingham	7	
Grenocle in Kent		in Kent [and Two Men		
2 men & 2 anchors,		in Armour with the		
with the ships of		ships of Hastings]		
Hastings		Bekesbourne in Kent	7	
Rye,	5	Town of Rye	5	
Winchelsea,	10	Winchelsea	10	Romenal, 3 ships, in each 21 men and a boy; to it pertain - Promehall, Lede Estwestone, Dengemaris and OldRomney
Romney,		Port of Romney	4	
& Old Romney,	4			
Lydde,	1	Lydde	7	
Hithe,	5	Port of Hythe	5	Hythe, 3 ships, as Romenal; to it pertains W Hythe
Dover,	19	Port of Dover	19	Dover, 21 ships as Hastings. To it pertain Folkestone, Faversham and St Margarets, not concerning the land, but for goods and chattels
Folston,	1	Town of Folkestone	7	
Faversham,	1	Town of Faversham	7	
Sandwich, Stonor,	5	Port of Sandwich, with	5	Sandwich, 5 ships as Romenal and Hythe. To it pertain Fordwich, Reculver, Serre, and Deal; not for the Soil, but for the Goods.
Fordwich, Dale,		Stonar, Fordwich,		
and Sarre,		Deal, etc		
A total of 57 ships ... on forty days' summons, and for each ship 20 men and a master, and every ship to be armed ... and fitted at the proper costs of the Cinque Ports - 15 days at the costs of the Ports, and after at the costs of the king, for which the master was to be paid 6d per day, Constable 6d, and the others 3d.		Sum of ships, 88; these ships on 40 days' summons all to be fitted out at the charge of the Ports, each to have a Master and 20 men, and to be maintained for 15 days at their own cost. - they were to be paid Master, 6d., Constable, 6d., per day and mariners 3d. and after these days, at the expense of the crown.		Sum of Ships 57, Men 1187, Boys 57. This service the Barons of the Five Ports do acknowledge as due to the King upon Summons yearly; if it happens by the space of 15 days together at their own costs and charges, accounting the first day as that upon which sails were spread to the King's destination, and to serve as long as necessary after at the King's expense.

The Sea-Service following the Charter of 1278

able to afford the construction of the new harbour necessitated by the progressive silting. The drainage of the Walland Marsh between the twelfth and sixteenth centuries, subsequent to that of Romney Marsh and known as the 'Innings', also contributed to the problems. Whereas Hythe Haven, New Romney, and other small ports in the vicinity had enjoyed generations of well accessible and sheltered facilities, these were dramatically curtailed.

The Ports still had a defensive role to play. They carried enormous influence and their solution to an otherwise intractable problem was to increase the number of Members; Seaford, Bulverhythe, Margate and Birchington joined voluntarily, and the great charter of Edward II confirmed numerous others together with the Cinque Ports' status of Rye, Winchelsea and Hythe. The informality of many of the arrangements is emphasised by the absence of an authoritative list of Members, until Simon de Pencestre as Lord Warden prepared one in 1293; at last, there was an exceptional administrator, and he was the one credited with fundamental reorganisation of the Castle and the fleets.

The Arms of the Cinque Ports

The smaller ships of the thirteenth century displayed few changes from the basic longboats, of which town seals and municipal arms are a crude source of illustration. That of Sandwich shows a Mediterranean influence with the deck beams projecting through the hull; that of Hythe displays a bowsprit, whilst that of la Rochelle shows reef points in the sail; others show the stern castles as still being of primitive construction, and with anchors comprising a net of stones slung from the bow. Among the earliest is that of Dover, predating even the college of Heralds; it shows the three royal lions *passant*, modified by their being halved with ships' hulls, a design which came to be common to the Cinque Ports. The seal of Hastings shows the prow of the English ship with the Royal Standard as a reminder of the Convention of Bruges in 1297, when it was agreed that English ships in Flemish waters should display *'le signal des armes du Roy d'Angleterre'*. The corporate seals of the other Ports are also among the earliest known, but there was not one common to the Ports as such until that ordered in 1613 for the Yarmouth bailiffs.

The Port of London had gained ascendancy over Sandwich by the end of the thirteenth century, and the crown was less willing to accept the Ports' traditional independence; even so, there was little that could be done to restrain either their piracy or their battles with Yarmouth. The continued growth of international trade embraced competition from the North Sea down to the south west, and impinged on the traditional fishing grounds; England's danger of losing its sovereignty of the seas called for a more substantial navy but, in this, the Ports' ships were of diminished use.

Richard's encounters with the Saracen fleets provided uncomfortable lessons in the use of a higher freeboard and a lateen rig for greater manoeuvrability, but these were not generally applied to the smaller ships at home. The increase in trade called for larger vessels and the ubiquitous *cog*, that had been around since the early thirteenth century, came into greater use; initially, this was a dumpy version of the double-ended longboat with a higher freeboard, and still mostly rowed; soon it was given a single mast stepped in a central open hold, and with decking fore and aft; this was a clumsy vessel, with a virtually flat bottom for landing perhaps thirty tons of cargo onto beaches, and its castles were built as a part of the hull instead of as mere superstructures; the near vertical stern made the rudder an obvious innovation, being more effective when the vessel heeled under the increasing use of sail power. The town seal of Rye, dating from around 1390, is one of the first depictions of a transome-mounted rudder; the sailing ability was also of importance, as depicted by the sailor manning the sheets. There also emerged the *hoy*, a handy single-masted all-purpose vessel; this appeared at many ports around the country, and indeed was similar to that used into the nineteenth century in continental Europe and as illustrated in numerous early paintings. Another design to emerge was that of the *balinger*, a two-masted vessel of sturdy construction with perhaps twenty pairs of oars, usually of 40-60 tons and favoured for the carriage of messengers; this however, seems to have been confined to the Cinque Ports.

The expansion in trade was reflected in the work of the Admiralty Court at Dover, whose functions included inquests on wrecks and captured ships, issuing licenses for passages, receiving customs dues, punishing offenders for offences committed at sea, summonsing Portsmen for their ship service and impressing additional ships as required. This level of activity encouraged the Ports to make greater use of their private courts of the Brodhull and the later Guestling.

The Brodhull was a formal affair concerned with the appointment of bailiffs to the Yarmouth Fair, the receiving of their reports and the settling of their accounts; in the Court's early days, each Head Port had elected its own bailiffs but only four were sent from 1360 onwards. The Guestlings originally served Hastings, Rye and Winchelsea, but subsequently the eastern Ports held their own; there was no established meeting place, and the name acknowledged the invitation to the non-corporate members; their hearings were directed at settling the allocation of ship service and payments in lieu, and occasionally the distribution of the spoils of their legalised piracy. The composition of these two local courts was pseudo-parliamentary; they sat under the direction of a speaker, and their success was due to immunity from the courts at Westminster.

The early part of the fourteenth century saw the great European famine and another pestilence affecting cattle but, although England was still a major exporter, they were lawless times. In 1314 the king authorised Winchelsea to equip two ships to defend the coast from pirates but, within a month, one of them had itself committed at least a half-dozen acts of piracy. He determined also to conclude the Scottish problem, and assembled his army at Newcastle; the undiminished status of the Ports encouraged them to provided a fleet in 1319, and this included a ship with a drop-bridge for storming city walls. The poor conduct of the campaign necessitated their help until its end in 1323, long beyond any accepted extension of ship service; this, together with erratic payment, led to disaffection with far-reaching consequences. Queen Isabella and her court had moved to Holland where she colluded with Mortimer; in the following year, they sailed intent on an invasion through East Anglia. The Cinque Ports' dislike of both the King and his appointed Lord Warden led to their providing no resistance, and the King was dethroned in 1327; thereafter the Ports became less involved with the royal fleets.

The reign of King Edward III opened with the country falling to numerous pressures, both at home and abroad, and one of the King's own ships was plundered at Sandwich in 1334. There was little opportunity for retaliation; the control of the channel was lost, and the French King declared forfeit the English territories of Gascony and Anjou. The only responses open to Edward were to reinforce his coastal castles, to build rapidly a fleet of larger ships, and to impress the support of the southern ports.

The hundred years war with France started in 1337 and, over the next couple of years, the French advantage over the channel waters improved steadily. They vented their deep resentment towards the Ports and mounted numerous raids; Southampton was overrun in 1338; Hastings, Rye, Folkestone, Winchelsea and Dover were targeted in the following year and, soon afterwards, every ship in Romney and Hythe was destroyed; in that year too, Edward was humiliated by having several of his own ships being seized in the North Sea. The Valois were building a major naval dockyard at Rouen and there was fear of an invasion; a tremulous Parliament declared the Cinque Ports to be discharged of all obligations including land duties, other than to 'keep guard and watch'.

The Ports recovered sufficiently by 1340 to assemble a fleet of twenty-one ships and these, together with others from the Thames, beat off a French attack on Hastings and Rye; the French were forced to retreat to Boulogne, which the English then raided with vigour. Later, a fleet of nearly two hundred French, Genoese and Spanish ships assembled off Sluys at the mouth of the Zwin, to bar the king's passage and blockade the Flemings; the fleet of the Ports, together with a further 70 vessels impressed from the western ports, reinforced the king's fleet; although this combination was vastly inferior to the ocean-going ships of the assembly, the twelve hours' battle was successful due to the superiority of the English archers.

Control of the channel was regained, but the underlying decline in the Ports could not be concealed and the King remitted one-half of the cost of the ships they had furnished. It proved to be the last major encounter they initiated and, even when the king renewed his campaign in France, only twenty-one ships of the Ports were impressed out of the total of 735 merchantmen employed. The Ports' contingent was small in size, but was balanced by the responsibility for lodging, victualling, and transporting the army, although they did receive a proportionately greater recompense for the storage of gunpowder and shot. The Ports were charged too, with relieving poor and distressed sailors, many of whom may have been shipwrecked, and with keeping watches through the night throughout the year, sometimes with as many as twelve at each port.

In 1348, the plague reached England from France; the outbreak peaked in the winter of 1349, was to recur with equal severity in the winter of 1361, and there were further outbreaks through the fifteenth century. The death toll is thought to have varied between twenty and fifty percent of the population, and the rat-infested ports probably suffered most. The resulting dearth of labour rapidly impacted on the agricultural economy, dramatically curtailed shipbuilding, and restricted both sides in the war with France. In 1350 it was not a French fleet, but a Castilian bringing merino wool to Flanders, that had taken advantage of the shortage of manpower and plundered English merchantmen in the channel. An assembly off Sandwich of fifty small vessels and pinnaces intercepted it near Dungeness on its return voyage; of the enemy ships, seventeen were captured and the remainder put to flight, but both the prince's ship and the *Thomas* were sunk.

The expeditions in France were soon resumed, and the victories did much to restore confidence. The economies in the south recovered on the back of wool and grain and, at the peak, some 30,000 sacks or eight million fleeces per annum were exported, and supported numerous valuable imports. Calais remained the English trading bridgehead for some two hundred years, and supported by a rolling ferry service from Dover that flourished as a result.

There was a vast expansion in the fish trade from the late 1320's, of which one-half of Yarmouth's exports alone reached 10 million fish, and with the majority for home consumption sold through middlemen. The London Fishermen's Guild was among the most powerful, and its members were particularly active at Yarmouth and Rye where they were substantial landowners. The efforts at local control included 'hosting', whereby freemen were encouraged to purchase facilities for the fishermen and their buyers, usually subject to the right to purchase a proportion of the catch, and this system was employed at Yarmouth, Rye, and New Romney. This large volume of trade provided impetus to the growth of all ports; London became the largest, with its monopolistic trading practices impinging on the Ports' ability to compete; the strength of London was followed closely by Southampton, leaving the Cinque Ports with limited importance in the southeast, and their only remaining commercial advantage lay in tax exemptions and their restricted ability to trade 'lovescope free'. The fights with Yarmouth continued, and the crown imposed a truce on terms that Yarmouth sought to exploit; the Ports made a coherent response through the Brodhull, which was removed to Romney for this purpose.

In the latter half of the fourteenth century the economy was depleted by further recurrences of the plague and severe storms. The English possessions in France were declared forfeit, and an invasion was again threatened; the shortage of manpower limited the size of the force despatched to Calais and it was forced to return. The French and Castilian raiders grew bolder and the war with France resumed, but the French navy had consolidated with disastrous consequences; Fowey, Plymouth, Melcombe Regis, Poole, Hastings, Rye, and Gravesend were all sacked, the mouth of the Thames had to be protected by booms, and the Yarmouth herring fleet was attacked. The invasion never materialised, and the English fisheries survived because their expeditions were limited to little more than three days in local waters, due to the difficulties in preserving catches. Trading however, was a different matter; the foreign ships were much larger, were monopolising the oceans, and were based beyond the Ports. The only remaining English advantages on the seas were a reputation for toughness and an intimate knowledge of the local waters.

In the meantime, Hastings was a victim of coastal erosion; New Winchelsea, Romney and Hythe were increasingly choked with shingle; Dover also required major efforts to avoid silting, to the extent that its cross-channel traffic had, at times, to be conducted off the beach; Stonar was washed away in the 1360's. Sandwich, which had been a major port failed towards the end of that century when silting closed the Wantsum channel. Hythe suffered from shipwrecks, fire and pestilence, and later would have been abandoned had King Henry IV not discharged it from ship service. The Ports' defensive role was coming to an end within an emerging navy, but they still mounted sufficient raids on the French coast to prevent too clear an advantage. They exercised their Honours at Court at the coronation of King Richard II in 1377; subsequently, the only notable service they performed in that century was the provision of royal transport.

The decline in their role led them to rely even more on their privileges, and they made many enemies at home; they resorted to economic piracy, and Parliament started questioning their exemption from taxes. Yarmouth declined as a fishing port in spite of its substantial trading fleet; the combination of war, silting of the harbour and changes in dietary preferences led to the withdrawal of London investments, and this was a pattern repeated in the Ports. When Sandwich closed as a major port and the commercial activities of Dover were restricted to a ferry service, international trade moved to the ever-expanding ports of London and Southampton. With debut of the compass, the appearance of rhumb lines on charts, and the establishment of seafaring codes, the Portuguese caravel made its appearance in English ports. This design combined the lateen sails of the Arab dhow with the square rig of the day, the larger vessels having square main and topsails on the foremast, and lateens on two further masts giving better performance when tacking; their displacement varied between 100 and 200 tons. These were vessels that the Ports were unable to match.

The Ports were now reduced to reliance on their privileges and, in this, the Brodhull was vital. Through it they fought the crown collection of any taxes and, in so far as they were payable, claimed the right to assess them for themselves. The right of the Portsmen to claim that all actions in which they were involved should be heard there, was a growing issue with the courts at Westminster; a Brodhull called by Hastings in 1436 decided that it would be in the common interest to reject a *subpoena* served on one of their members by an exterior court; in 1437, it was ordered by the Brodhull that *'no resident of the Ports or their members shall sue any other resident in any other court out of the liberties of the five Ports* [and] *anyone doing so shall be fined 10li ... '*; there were numerous orders in a like vein, including one of 1461 in which it was held that any town troubled by the *'mynyster of the Castell of Dover'* was to have his costs shared among all the Ports. These were rearguard actions, but they maintained a modicum of success into the 1600's; the Brodhull and Guestlings were merged in 1633 into the 'Brotherhood and Guestling', although many different spellings of 'Brotherhood' were used in the minutes.

The fifteenth century expansion of inshore fishing in the south-west attracted fleets from the Ports and from Brittany, and the western fishermen paid tolls at Lydd, Rye and Winchelsea. The French made their presence felt at Yarmouth, and the Ports were again exposed to retaliatory raids that included the sacking of Sandwich in 1457; their piratical responses made them an embarrassing defensive necessity, but they retained their influence in the southeast by the exercise of a reign of terror.

In 1461, the Ports again exercised their Honours at Court; *'... the Lord Edward the fourth was exalted to be king of England and was crowned at Westminster and the barons of the Ports bore the canopy as of custom. The cloth drapings of the spears and canopy pertain to Romney and Dover and shall be divided between them this time. They shall pertain to Sandwich and Hythe the next time'*. In 1465, the king sought to bribe them into some degree of conformity with the grant of a new Charter, but the placing of the Portsmen beyond any sanction outside their own jurisdiction encouraged them even further into piracy; they were playing little part in the navy, other than as a transport fleet which later carried Henry VII to and from France in 1491. There emerged the problems of poor fishing, decaying ports, and weak state power; indeed, it was only the continued exemption from taxes that sustained some of the smaller and impoverished Ports; by 1488, the Portsmen were reduced to paying for convoy protection appointed by the crown.

The accession of King Henry VII was to a poor economy. King Henry VIII therefore inherited a piecemeal navy and poor defences against France and Spain, whose invasion plans targeted Pevensey, Hastings, Winchelsea and Rye yet again. His response was to construct numerous defensive castles, and many of the sites of their supporting chain of beacons dated from early Saxon times. Whilst the standard of cartography had changed little over the previous two hundred years, his maps of the defensive surveys of the coast were highly sophisticated in that they were deliberately distorted to emphasise the most important features.

The construction and subsequent garrisoning of defences on the south coast contributed to local economies, but the Ports were little involved; the silting of harbours precluded their being considered either for the new naval dockyards or for accommodating the larger ships carrying cannons. Some of the smaller Ports had also to resort to chartering ships of the required tonnage to fulfil their service as, in 1514, Romney chartered four ships from Hastings.

There still was neither distinction between heavily armed merchantmen and men-of-war, nor any defined battle order. Henry addressed these shortcomings with the construction of dedicated naval vessels in specialised dockyards, thus bringing to an end the Ports' strategic influence; their ships were insignificant when compared with the new *Grace a Dieu* of 1,000 tons. In 1513 therefore, the Ports' only use was to assist in the transport of the King and his army to France, but their historic status was acknowledged by instructions that their men should wear *'a cote of whyte cotyn with a red cross and the arms of the Portis undeneath; that is to say, halfe lyon and halfe ship'*; this possibly was the first naval uniform, but it was insufficient to disguise the Ports' reduced importance. Even when there was the great gathering of ships at Dover in 1520 for the meeting between Henry and Francis I at the 'Field of Gold', only a token force from the Ports was present.

The scramble for defence rebounded on the fishing industry to the extent that the home market required protection. The price of fish was fixed within a radius of Yarmouth and the Portsmen were fined for selling elsewhere; in 1550, however, they were excused because *'the Rode at the seid town Yarmouth is not good but very daungerous in the time of tempest and foul weather'*. Seven years later, the further decline led to the Brodhull declaring *'For that there is warres that almost none of our Fysshermen of the portes wylbe at Yermoth this yere wherefore it is agreed that there shall be but too bailifes go to Yermoth this present yere and so from henceforth'*.

The Ports claimed their Honours at Court at the coronation of Queen Elizabeth I and, typically, there arose a dispute among them as to the proceeds of the canopy, staves and bells; as a result, the trophies were sold and the proceeds divided. The new Queen was minded to curtail their privileges, which she regarded as an expensive luxury in terms of taxation at least, but she made no progress against them except in so far as the Portsmen made greater defensive efforts. She resisted a claim by Sandwich for financial support when a stranded ship blocked the harbour, but that town did receive her encouragement to accept the victims of European religious persecution, and new industries followed.

A General Brotherhood held at Romney on Tuesday, 25 July 1570, cited the Statute of Herrings and proclaimed the duties of the bailiffs at the Yarmouth fair; it, set out for the first time what may conveniently be described as bylaws relating to the conduct of the Portsmen in attendance, but made it clear that *'no encroachment is to be made against the strond and den of the barons of the Ports at Yarmouth'*. The bylaws included such matters as a prohibition on the wearing of armour and the imposition of curfews, and extended to rules regarding the sale of fish, assizes of bread, and fixing the maximum prices of ales. The judicial procedure was precise, and some 34 specific punishments were listed including *'for stealing fishing tackle, or otherwise from boats, on the first offence, 40 days; on the second, 6 months; on the third, hanging'*, *'for finding a body at sea or on the shore and not declaring the goods, shall be fined their value and imprisoned'*, *'for cutting off anchor buoys, and the ship be lost as a result, hanging'*; their acceptance of a wider order of conduct was reflected in *'for carrying staple goods beyond customized ports, without license, fined to the value of the goods'*, *'for carrying felons or their goods to a place beyond the sea shall forfeit his ship'*, and *'for hiring a foreign ship, when an English one was available, fining'*; here too, was the commencement of ordered conservation, in that *'for taking oysters or mussels between May 1 and September 14, or young fry with nets with eyes too small, a grievous fine'*, *'for fishing for plaice and sols with mashes or mokes less than five inches, all such nets forfeited, and fined'*, *'for fishing for plaice or sols between November 1 and March 15, fine 40s for each offence'* and with an unusually neat touch, *'for fishing between sunset and sunrise and won't suffer the Fish quietly to enjoy their Night's Feed - 40s'*.

The last great offensive in which the Ports were involved was in repelling the Spanish Armada; their small contingent, each with an attendant pinnace of 30 tons, was at the total cost of £4,300. It comprised, from Hastings the *Anne Bonaventure* of 70 tons and a crew of 49 together with eleven small vessels as tenders; from Romney the *John* of 60 tons; from Rye, the *William* of 80 tons; from Hythe, only a pinnace; from Dover, the *Elizabeth* [or *Elnathan*] of 120 tons together with five fire ships which were not used; from Sandwich, the *Reuben* of 110 tons, and from Faversham the *Hazard* of 38 tons. This limited contribution provided good service and, on one account, a ship of Dover decoyed the *Galleas* of Spain and put her on the ground near Calais where they burned her.

The Confederation had little more to offer beyond its seafaring skills; these remained in strong demand by the new professional navy, but conditions were so poor that the Press Gangs became necessary. There was no provision for the families left behind, and even the minimal payments to the impressed seamen were withheld if the ship was lost. There was the inevitable result of escape from the gangs that encouraged a life of smuggling; it reached gigantic proportions in the eighteenth and nineteenth centuries along much of the coast from Sussex to Thanet; it was estimated in 1779 that, of the four million gallons of gin annually distilled at Schiedam alone, most was smuggled to England.

King James I recognised the decayed state of the Ports, and granted them new charters in 1604; these affirmed the privileges of holding courts of record, of trying all actions real and personal, and of the retention of fines; they were also granted the right to raise taxes and were exempted from those of the Crown. This grant coincided with a depression in the Norwegian fishing industry, to which the Dutch responded by expanding their own; they used fleets of even larger vessels, the *busses*, and also developed salt-curing at sea. The English fishing industry continued to decline, and this was also reflected in the commercial fleets.

King Charles I was forced to raise taxes as best he could, to support his continuing wars. To that end he demanded ship money for the first time in 1634; the Ports, other than Rye, ignored this. In 1637, he made his third demand; the Ports succumbed but claimed some remission, saying that there was not a single fishing boat at New Romney or Lydd and only a few at Hythe; even Rye, which had made great attempts to retain its harbour, was reduced to writing to the other Ports for aid. It was the Royal mismanagement, culminating in defeat by the Scots and the commencement of the great Irish rebellion, that led to civil war.

On the restoration of the monarchy, the Ports again claimed their Honours at Court, but there was an indecorous fight between the Portsmen and the King's footmen, and the King himself had to intervene. This token intervention on their behalf could not conceal their ever-diminishing importance and economic decline which brought to an end their infighting and riotous state of affairs with Yarmouth; in 1632, they carried their banner to the Herring Fair for the last time. There were further charters granted in the seventeenth century that reaffirmed many of their rights, but these were only of nominal importance, and their status was now little more than the tradition of their honours at court; they surrendered their charters in 1668.

The Ports retained idiosyncrasies in local government, and they manipulated these to maintain an oligarchic control; gerrymandering was rife to the extent that Sandwich was for a while disenfranchised. Parliament brought them to conformity with the rest of the country in the mid twentieth century, but nevertheless with a later provision to secure continuation of the Confederation. The office of Warden of the Cinque Ports survives as an honorary title, with the benefit of the official residence of Walmer Castle; since the last war, the office has been variously conferred on Sir Winston Churchill, H.M. the Queen Mother, and Admiral Lord Boyce.

The present membership comprises the head ports of Hastings, New Romney, Hythe, Dover and Sandwich, and the two 'Antient Towns' of Rye and Winchelsea; the additional members are Tenterden, Deal, Faversham, Folkestone, Lydd, Ramsgate, Margate and Brightlingsea. The Port of Dover alone has maintained its original identity, whilst the others have adapted or declined. There remains a fascinating collection of communities, many of which retain a strong maritime flavour, and many with townscapes and a wealth of history meriting exploration.

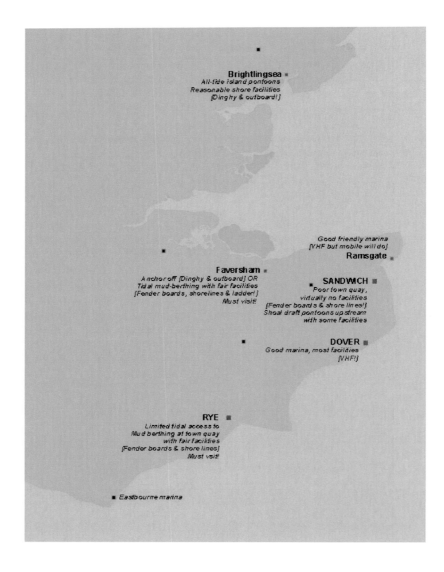

Brightlingsea
All-tide island pontoons
Reasonable shore facilities
[Dinghy & outboard!]

Good friendly marina
[VHF but mobile will do]
Ramsgate

Faversham
Anchor off [Dinghy & outboard] OR
Tidal mud-berthing with fair facilities
[Fender boards, shorelines & ladder!]
Must visit!

SANDWICH
Poor town quay,
virtually no facilities
[Fender boards & shore lines!]
Shoal draft pontoons upstream
with some facilities

DOVER
Good marina, most facilities
[VHF!]

RYE
Limited tidal access to
Mud berthing at town quay
with fair facilities
[Fender boards & shore lines]
Must visit!

Eastbourne marina

The 'Navigable Ports'

THE NAVIGABLE PORTS

THERE REMAINS a half dozen only of the Ports and their Members still sensibly and interestingly navigable for the yachtsman by sail or motor; even among these, the accessibility and berthing vary widely. Ramsgate and Dover have their modern marinas, whilst Rye, Sandwich and Faversham have restricted tidal gates and quayside mud berthing; Brightlingsea falls somewhere in between.

They provide an attractive group for a fifteen-days' exploration for shoal draft craft of up to, say, ten metres; this is admittedly hard-going and weather-dependent, and it would be understandable if mariners from the west omitted Brightlingsea; a suggested tide-dependent itinerary is appended. Regrettably, vessels unable to take to the mud will have to content themselves with Dover, Ramsgate and Brightlingsea, although anchoring in the Swale can be a good option for Faversham. An RYA 'Day Skipper' prepared to work the tides should not find the navigation unduly demanding; the craft should be equipped with VHF, depth sounder, GPS, and up-to-date charts and pilotage. Fender boards and shore lines are essential at Rye, Sandwich and Faversham; a dinghy is near essential at Brightlingsea and, of course, also at Faversham if anchoring off. It is always worthwhile making an advance telephone call to the Harbourmaster or Yard before setting off, especially for the smaller destinations.

These Ports provide unique attractions in their ambience, and it will be hard to resist the temptation not to move on, even if the berthing facilities are not as expected by some. The short excursion options are introductions to the towns with the one-day visitor in mind, the pub and restaurant suggestions are just that, with the near guarantee of making a return visit.

The Ypres Castle Museum and Gun Garden

The Ypres Castle merits a history of its own. It was probably built by The Lord Warden, Peter of Savoy, under a commission of King Henry III in 1249 as the principal defence of the town, and originally was known as the Badding's Tower. It passed into private ownership with the ending of the French raids; it was subsequently repurchased by the Corporation, and used successively as a meeting place, town gaol and museum.

RYE

RYE, apart from being merely interesting, is a medieval experience. The town is 3nM from the harbour entrance on a cliff above the coastal marshlands, and provides a unique cluster of narrow streets and fine architecture, all with a wealth of history; it is a major tourist attraction with corresponding advantages and disadvantages. The tidal access to the harbour is not difficult, and mud berthing alongside the Strand Quay is at the foot of the town centre itself.

History

The town is unusual among the Ports, in that the absence of spring water discouraged any permanent settlement until the tenth century; from then until the mid-nineteenth century, it was a predominantly maritime community. Looking down from the town today it is apparent that the coastline has changed, but the extent is difficult to imagine. In early times, the River Rother cut a 200m wide estuary through coastal marshes backed by dense woodland; some two miles inland, there was the confluence of the Rivers Rother, Brede and Tillingham, all of which were navigable in varying degrees. In 893 the Danes sent 250 of their boats up the old course of the River Rother towards Appledore; it is not surprising that, in this sparsely populated region, it took considerable efforts to displace them.

The sandstone promontory rising above the marshes was an obvious landmark, but it was described as merely lying within the manors of Ramslie and Brede, and was granted by Canute to the Abbey of Fécamp in Normandy; unusually, only a proportion of the revenues were granted, and not the full manorial rights. It was from this time that the ports of Old Winchelsea and Broomhill grew, guarding the west and east of the river mouth respectively; the channels were tortuous, with the later port of Iham on the River Brede being two miles to the *southwest* of Rye, and extensive sea walls had by then been raised to protect the marshland grazing. Old Winchelsea and its superb harbour were inundated by 1280, and New Winchelsea was established on the heights above Iham but its harbour was abandoned in the sixteenth century.

The charter of Edward the Confessor nominated the five ports individually. Rye and Winchelsea were attached as Members of Hastings, and Rye's town seal then made its first appearance as the oldest known of any in the Confederation. In the twelfth century, Rye and Winchelsea jointly contributed two ships to Hastings but, by 1190, that port was in decline; of its provision of twenty-one ships, Rye then provided five and

Winchelsea ten. Rye's shipbuilding was already notable; it provided a haven for some of the king's galleys, where they were laid up between 1237 and 1243 at the new and enlarged dockyard, and in 1243, the royal galleys of Sandwich and Romney were directed there. There were two further galleys built between 1259 and 1261, and *'two balingers each of twenty oars'* as late as 1377; sail power was taking over by this time, and these balingers would have been very 'old technology', indicative of the limitations of local industry. The town of Tenterden is upstream; eventually it was a Limb of Rye, and was served by the port and major shipbuilding yard at Smallhythe.

The charter of the Abbey of Fécamp, of about 1150, illustrates the importance of the town's fisheries; through this a fixed proportion of every catch was levied, and this varied with the size of boat. In 1305 the town petitioned for the annual fair, held on the eighth September [the Feast of the Nativity of the Virgin Mary], to be brought forward to the 15th August [the Feast of the Assumption] *'because all ... are at sea engaged in fyshing'*; this was granted, notwithstanding the date having been fixed from 1190. The local economy, of course, benefited from the secondary industries; these included sail making, rope spinning, and the making of fishing hooks, and there were many exports to other regions.

The Church of St Mary from Lion Street

The Abbots of Fécamp were responsible for the magnificent town church of St. Mary. The building was completed in about 1190, of richly ornamented cathedral quality, and remains a superb example of the sense of dedication of the day. It was at the centre of community life, used for secular as well as religious celebrations, and was the venue too, for many religious plays.

King Richard I granted the first license to fortify the town, and granted the town's revenues to defray the cost, but subject to a penalty of £100 if the walls were not built within three years; the fortifications were by no means completed, but there is no record as to whether the penalty was imposed. In the time of King John, the French occupied the town when they overran southern England. King Henry III in 1247 reclaimed the grant to Fécamp for reasons of national security; he gave them lands in the manor of Cheltenham in exchange, and took direct control of the town under the charge of a Royal Bailiff. This arrangement was short lived, and the King granted the rights to the Barons for an annual payment and their accepting responsibility for the sea defences.

The progressive decline of Hastings was matched by the expansion of Rye and Winchelsea. In 1272 therefore, King Edward I granted them both a charter, thus giving them Cinque Port equivalency under the style of the *'Two Antient Towns'*; the lands to the west of the town had remained with the Abbey, and hence that settlement was referred to as 'Rye Foreign' as situated outside the jurisdiction of the town and Ports. Rye and Winchelsea, after their incorporation, each found in alternate years one bailiff for the Yarmouth Fair and, in the fourteenth century, Rye was still receiving rents from Yarmouth.

In 1275 Edward granted the town's manorial rights to his mother, Queen Eleanor, who appointed her own bailiff although with little impact on the day to day running of the town. Already, there were elected jurats, but it was not until after her death that there is the first mention of an appointed mayor; he governed jointly with the bailiff, and was supported by the much earlier elected jurats. By 1307, the appointment of bailiff was little more than honorary and, in 1705, the town's Corporation assumed the function of both offices; there remains the custom of the mayor to this day holding two maces. The established procedure was for the mayor to be elected from among the barons, following which he chose his own twelve jurats, from whom the office of town clerk was then elected.

The growth of Rye and Winchelsea did nothing to inhibit their piratical activities. They are recorded as having looted the goods of Gascon merchants to the huge value of £11,000, but the attempted investigation by the Lord Warden was physically prevented, and the pirates escaped charges. There were other incidents in which the Corporation refused to surrender those involved; they not only pleaded the immunity of the Cinque Ports, but also refused to impart local justice.

The natural defences of the seaward facing cliff were sufficient for generations. Whilst the Cinque Ports were at their zenith in the thirteenth century, there was little exposure to attack from the landward side. The additional defence of the Baddings Tower is of uncertain origin; it was later acquired by the Corporation and used variously as a meeting place and gaol into the late nineteenth century, with an intervening period in the ownership of one John de Ypres.

In the storm of 1284, the River Rother filled up at the mouth and made its new and shorter course through Rye; this finally turned to Rye's advantage in the great storm of 1287 when much of old Winchelsea was destroyed. Rye's importance then grew further for fishing, boat building and channel crossings; in 1300, it provided a substantial force for service in the war against Scotland.

The French control of the channel in the fourteenth century occasioned the commissioning of further town defences in 1329. These included the construction of the town walls on the north side, and the costs were to be subsidised by the King Edward III in the form of murage grants; few of these works were put in hand, and the French raids began in earnest in around 1330 as a prelude to the commencement of the Hundred Years War. This was marked by a French fleet which, driven off from Sandwich, invaded Rye; the fleet of the Cinque Ports chased them off, carried out a retaliatory attack on Boulogne, and hanged the French captains. In 1339, the town was again attacked by the French and the fleet of the Cinque Ports fleet put to sea as a prelude to the battle at Sluys; of the mere twenty vessels, four were from Rye - the *Michael* of 240 tons, the *Nicholas* of 120 tons, and the *Palmere* and the *Edmond* each of 60 tons. Although the town managed to send nine ships for the siege of Calais in 1347, the French raids must have caused considerable damage, because it was reported that 52 houses and a mill remained burned and uninhabitable.

In 1340 the Landgate was built but, in the same year, the lower parts of the town were inundated. A further petition to the Crown in 1348 claimed that *'whereas their town is surrounded on all sides by the sea a great part of the town has been consumed by the sea and in other ways, and the total destruction of the town is feared unless the same be speedily strengthened, especially since the town is situated in a place where the enemies' galleys come more frequently than elsewhere on the coast'*. The marshlands to the north of the town had made fortification on that side unnecessary. This changed with the innings but, even by 1369, few of the town's defences had been built; eventually, serious efforts were made, resulting for the most part in a simple earth embankment extending from the Landgate to the western Strand Gate, and partly complemented with a ditch to the northwest sector. This however, coincided with the arrival of the Black Death, and the shortage of manpower and the town's difficulties were compounded in 1375 by a cliff fall on the east side, and the northeast side of the town was washed away below a line between the Ypres Tower and the Landgate.

The Landgate

The reciprocal cross-channel raids were not all politically motivated, and the background to the French raid of 1377 is illustrative. Ships from each of Rye and France were watering at the same spring in Normandy, and the crews came to blows as to which should have the first fill; a French sailor was killed and the Rye ship sailed off, but a Boulogne crew slaughtered that of another English ship, hanging the bodies from the yards, interspersed with those of dogs; Rye then initiated a coast-harrying expedition with the result of a particularly ferocious response in which the French took their church bells and then moved on to pillage the Isle of Wight; in the following year, Rye and Winchelsea combined to do likewise, and recovered the bells together with a great deal of plunder.

The town was remarkably resilient in the face of the many catastrophes, and it remained a major port into the 1380's for both continental and home trade. The forests were exploited for shipbuilding and firewood and these exports were matched by the imports of oil, spices, cider and straw products, and there was a flourishing wine trade with Gascony. The pottery works were also established in that century, using fine quality local clays, and there were five kilns operating until the fifteenth century; their work is much sought-after by collectors; the pottery was resurrected in the eighteenth century in Ferry Road by the award winning Frederick Mitchell, and this became the Rye Pottery of today.

The French raids of 1385 led to the near-collapse of commerce; the export of firewood dropped to about a quarter of its peak, and the Gascony wine trade survived only to the end of the century. The impoverishment met with the common response of an increase in piracy, which was to continue through the century. In 1410, the town's burgesses were charged with maintaining an anti-piracy patrol in the channel; one of the burgesses turned pirate but, although imprisoned in the Tower of London, he was pardoned and was returned to parliament.

The town made a slow recovery during the fifteenth century; St. Mary's was rebuilt to its former standard, and many new houses were built outside the town walls; space within the town began to command a premium, and there was some reorganisation of its layout. Recovery was interrupted by further outbreaks of the plague and, after another sacking by the French in 1448, it was unable to fulfil its ship service. The Crown's response was much to the point, in that the remaining members of the Corporation were found to have been in dereliction of duty and were executed, but in 1449 Rye was granted Tenterden as a member to assist in the cost of ship service.

The stability associated with the end of the Hundred Years Wars enabled the resumption of growth, which was assisted by the acceptance of immigrant labour; the Corporation also received an income from its rent roll and local taxes, sufficient for its modest undertakings. The harbour was improved but silting soon reduced its availability; the problem might have been containable, but the inning of the marshes badly reduced scouring by the rivers, and caused deep conflicts between landowners and port users.

Rye was still stripping the forests for the export of firewood but, in the time of Henry VII, it was observed that *'the hoys that were laden with timber went out of Rye harbour to the number of thirty-seven on one tide, and never an English mariner among them'*. The town still owned a merchant fleet, possibly employed in the wine trade, but there are no records of its size; it may well be that these were the same ones as supplied the ship service, but calamity struck when the whole fleet went missing off Bordeaux, and it was never replaced.

Rye had one of the best harbours in the region at the beginning of the sixteenth century, with shelter for as many as 400 ships; by 1520, it was the most important town in Sussex, with rapidly growing revenues. The main sources of income were rents receivable, the greater 'box' comprising the quarterly dues paid by fishermen and the town tradesman, and the lesser 'box' from dues on goods and people passing through the port; these 'boxes' were similar to the 'droits' exacted in other towns. Expenditure grew similarly on defences, harbour repairs and conduits for the town's water supply; the first water cistern was installed in the churchyard at about this. In spite of these improvements, the town remained one with poor sanitation and inadequate water supply, and it was open to the influenza epidemics of 1555-6.

The Reformation was, for the most part, accepted by the Portsmen who had long been receptive to reformist ideas from the continent. There were only the two monastic institutions to be subjected to dissolution; the Hospital of St. Bartholomew, erected by the monks at Playden, was disbanded and replaced by the Corporation which purchased a second-hand building and erected it at the foot of Rye Hill; the other casualty was the small order of Austin Friars, settled since 1374, and whose seal was the earliest non-corporate one to show the arms of the Cinque Ports. On a lighter note, the quality of Rye fish was well recognised, because it was specifically ordered for the banquet at Dover on the arrival of Anne of Cleves.

John Fletcher was the noteworthy mayor and entrepreneur of 1530, and is thought to have spied against the French for Cardinal Wolsey. His real interest was in ship design and, having revolutionised windward performance with sails trimmed fore and aft, he passed his designs onto the royal dockyards; he was also the builder of *The Grand Mistress* of Rye, at 450 tons. There was as much need of improved defences at Rye as elsewhere and, to this end, Henry built the fortification of Camber Castle on the coastal plain below Winchelsea; unfortunately, almost before the castle was completed, the sea receded and the defences were superfluous.

The mainstays of the town's economy were fishing and trade. Fishing the more labour intensive and accounted for the employment of almost half the households; the Fishmarket was built in The Strand, but here the royal purveyor had the first choice. The harbour continued its major export of timber billets, together with horses mainly to Dieppe, and cloth to Rouen. It became a major distribution centre for imports of coal from Newcastle, and of salt, wine, and tobacco; in the first half of the century, there were also imports of Flemish bricks and, occasionally, grain. The port was also the main staging post with Dieppe, and sometimes for the Royal messengers. The shipyards remained an important industry, although this was mainly for smaller craft at the ports of Smallhythe and

Street near Tenterden. This economic growth was accompanied by the appearance of a new merchant class, with new properties built around the churchyard, in Market Street and in Middle [later Mermaid] Street; the poor settled around the low-lying area known as the Wash, and also around the Fishmarket and in Watchbell Ward. In the late sixteenth century, the combined tonnage of Rye's merchant shipping was about one-twelfth of that of London, but its pre-eminence among the Ports was more a reflection upon the Ports generally rather than a ground for Rye's complacency.

There were two recurring problems with Rye Harbour in the reign of King Edward VI. The first was silting, not only as a result of the continued innings, but also because of the practice of ships' masters dumping ballast; this was specifically addressed by a prohibiting Act of 1550. The second was that of the regional shipbuilding industry that was unable to compete with overseas yards in the size of vessels; thus, up to the late 1500's, most English ships were confining themselves to coastal trade, whilst foreign fleets were larger and able to trade with bigger ships in more distant waters.

The harbour problems continued; the new Queen Elizabeth was petitioned for assistance, and again in 1567 by the seamen and penned by Raleigh, but with no result. The town maintained its status in spite of the reappearance of economic problems and, in 1573, the Queen was sufficiently impressed on the occasion of her visit that she named it 'Rye Royal'. She declined to support the harbour but, as with Sandwich, she encouraged the immigrant Protestants to settle; in 1562, they numbered over 1,500 and their new industries did much to maintain the town's economy.

The Ports were overtaken by many others around the coast and, in 1587, the Queen threatened to withdraw their privileges because of their lack of defensive contribution; indeed, most of the town's guns were withdrawn and sent off to Tilbury. This royal outburst subsided with recognition of its inherently important defensive role; towards the end of the century, the defences were improved to include the erection of bulwarks and cannons on Strand Quay, and the purchase of the Gun Garden below the Ypres Tower.

When the Armada came, the town was well supplied with ordnance, and there was also the town's own-trained band of archers. The town had few ships of over 40 tons, but it did provide one of 69 tons under the command of Captain William Coxson and Master Edward Beale, together with a crew of fifty men and two boys; its armament included two pieces of brass and two fowlers, together with extensive provisions; possibly it was only a supply ship, because it is thought to have remained in port for the action. In the following year, the town's inability to accommodate the larger vessels for maritime defence was attributed to the innings; however, in 1596 the locally owned *Hercules* of 150 tons was fitted out for the expedition to Cadiz.

Rye was peaceful in the latter part of the sixteenth century. Its fleet had grown, and it continued to contribute its share of ship service; the annual cost was later calculated at more than £800 p.a., which was a substantial part of the town's revenues, and at a variance with the concept of the crown's generous treatment of the Ports. The population in 1580 had reached 4,500, with the economic mainstays of fishing and trading; between 1575 and 1595, Rye ships were making two annual catches at the distant Yarmouth and Scarborough, with an average of twenty five boats manned by a total of 324 men and boys; most of the catch was sold away, but that which was shipped home supported the industries of pickling and the barrelling of sprats and herrings.

The plague recurred in 1563, 1579-80 and again in 1596-97; it took about a third of the population, and the town was in a slow decline from the 1580's; the acceleration towards the end of the century was evidenced by the fall in the billett trade from 1,000,000 in 1558, to barely 200,000 in the 1590's. The unsuccessful attempts at harbour improvement, in spite of continued expenditure, reduced its capacity by nearly ninety percent; it was reflected in the decay of the fishing fleet, and exacerbated by the fall in consumption of fish following the Reformation. The harbour expenditure had necessitated a substantial increase in local taxation, and many of the wealthy left as a result; the fall in population was accelerated by the return home of many of the immigrant Protestants following increased religious tolerance.

The successions of Kings Henry and Edward, and Queens Mary and Elizabeth, saw numerous changes and conflicts in the parish church of St. Mary. This church fared better than many, as it had long been a parish rather than monastic establishment; from the 1550's, the Corporation was progressively reformist and, by 1571, thoroughly so with the appointment of a town preacher. The many works of art, vestments and plate were sold off, but they were at least applied to improvements to the church.

The seventeenth century opened with Rye's harbour in further decline; it was saved by its fishing and boat building industries although, by 1620, even the quantity of fish sold was down to one-third of that fifty years earlier; conversely, the town's economy was assisted by the increased area of agricultural land. There were numerous proposals for improvement of the harbour, including one for a new channel of almost two miles to the sea from between Camber Castle and Winchelsea; as this would have benefited Winchelsea more than Rye, it was abandoned. In 1627 and 1629, money for harbour improvements was raised by royal license and it was collected from much of southern England; the efforts were hampered by the absence of a full Harbour Board, and by the town's limited geographical jurisdiction. Thus, whilst the harbour still maintained two entrance channels at the opening of the century, by 1677 only one remained and its low-water depth was reduced to little over three metres.

That century produced three noteworthy figures in the town. It was early in the century that John Allen, a freeman of Rye, was instrumental in the construction of the first lighthouse at Dungeness. In 1636, the Elizabethan pattern of Grammar Schools was followed; the jurat Thomas Peacocke founded what is now the Old Grammar School in the High Street and, on his death, he left it and an endowment to the Corporation; it was a free school, and its articles provided for the master to be well versed in Latin and Greek, as well as his being barred from membership of the Corporation, but the pupils at that time were taught only the '3Rs' and navigation. In the late seventeenth century, the town was fortunate in its appointment of Jeakes as town clerk; he is best known for the seminal reference work *'Charters of the Cinque Ports, two Ancient Townes and their Members'*, and his family continued as important traders.

In 1634 and 1639, King Charles I endeavoured to levy ship money at £50 from each port; many refused, but Rye was one of the few fully to comply. At the outbreak of the Civil War in 1642, Rye readily declared itself for Parliament and looked to its defences; in the event, they were not tested, although the Royals ransacked one of the Dieppe passage boats. The Corporation quickly adopted the Engagement Act, requiring all in authority to sign a solemn undertaking to be true and faithful to the government *'without a King or House of Lords'*; the copies of these Engagements for most towns were destroyed on the Restoration, but Rye's was the only one to survive, signed by 168 jurats, freemen and tradesmen. In 1651, soldiers were garrisoned there at the town's expense for the Civil war; this was to cause considerable discontent because, in 1654, many attempted to set up business in competition with the town's traders to the detriment of an already depressed economy.

There were ensuing problems in the town's administration; these resulted in the Crown's encouragement of a restriction on the number of freemen to those wealthy enough to be accountable; the number came to be frozen, and this state of affairs continued until the commencement of the Municipal Reforms Acts of the nineteenth century. The effect in the eighteenth century was to concentrate membership of the Corporation into the hands of a few ruling families; for over one hundred years, with few exceptions, the mayoralty was held by the four inter-related families of the Lambs, Grebells, Slades and Davises. The conduct of the ruling families engendered resentment among the trades people who were allowed little say in the town's management. In 1743, John Breads the butcher sought to murder Lamb the Mayor as he walked past the churchyard at night; on that occasion however, Lamb had lent his distinctive coat to Allen Grebbell, his brother-in-law, who was murdered by mistake. The chartered rights of the town's courts left Breads to appear before Lamb as judge, with the inevitable result of the death sentence; justice of the day was clearly done because, at the trial, Breads merely expressed regret at not having succeeded; neither was justice harshly imposed because, instead of the Corporation claiming Bread's estate, it applied it to the benefit of his children.

The area of the Romney Marshes had been rife with smuggling from the sixteenth century; the numerous inlets and poor communications by land were ideal territory, and Rye was one of the more notorious centres. The Revenue cutters were insufficiently armed and manned to counter the numerous and blatantly active smugglers, one of the worst of which was the Hawkhurst gang frequently seen at the Mermaid Hotel; many used the interlinked attics of the houses to make their escape, and these attics remain today. There were numerous pitched battles between the excise men and the smugglers, and the last of these was in Rye Bay as late as 1826.

From 1680 Rye had been a Head Port for the collection of customs dues, its jurisdiction extending from Beachy Head to one mile east of the harbour entrance and, in 1848, this was extended to include Dungeness. In 1690, the French attempted yet another major incursion; they sent small vessels in to take soundings, but the harbour was saved by its inadequate depth of water for manoeuvring. Increasing volumes of commercial shipping during the seventeenth century called for improvements, but there was little done until the Rye leaders obtained authorisation by an Act of Parliament in 1724. There was an ambitious scheme, devised by Captain Perry, to provide a new harbour of some 60m width, extending over a third of a mile inland, and to be scoured by a sluice from the River Brede; unfortunately, three years later, the result was totally inadequate and the old harbour was re-opened on much the same course as the rivers follow today. It was not until the early nineteenth century, that the mouth of the river was recut and provided with a pier and wharfing on the eastern side, but the result was not very successful.

The French attack had encouraged the town to have better regard to its defences; guns were placed at the harbour entrance, and the Gun Garden was held in a state of readiness, with strict 'watch and ward' being kept. In the mid eighteenth century however, the old fortifications were not only in severe disrepair, but were increasingly inhibitive of the town's expansion; the portcullis was therefore removed from the Landgate, the Postern and Strand gates were widened and the stone from part demolition of the walls was used to surround the churchyard.

In 1800, small boat patrols were instigated in response to the Napoleonic threat, and warning beacons prepared. Nelson was recalled from the Baltic to take command of the squadron guarding the coast between Orford Ness and Beachy Head, and he chose to use Dungeness instead of the Downs as his focus; the lee of Dungeness was seen as an obvious landing place for French barges, and his position also reduced the possibility of his being held by the prevailing south westerlies. The further and major defence was the construction of the Royal Military Canal, backed by a military road from Rye to Hythe, as a means of reducing the length of the shore defences; this was commenced in 1804 and completed in 1806.

The constitution of the Corporation had continued unchanged with, in 1831, only twelve registered electors; the ensuing local riots were followed by the Reform Acts which enfranchised all with property to the value of £10 or more. The reforms did not proceed smoothly however, as the vacuum left by the withdrawal of the Lamb family was filled by Jeremiah Smith; he held control for some thirty years, until he was found guilty of corruption. Rye remained predominantly a market town, and fishing and commercial port, which handled large volumes of corn, coal, hops, oak-bark, timber and wool. There were substantial shipbuilding yards extending from the Town Quay up to and beyond Rock Channel, with the two largest shipbuilders of Hoad Bros and Hersell & Holmes at Strand Quay, the latter building the first steamer, the *William*, which was launched in 1857; the vessels were mostly coasters and fishing vessels of around 200 tons, but even later work failed to maintain Rye as a port of significance in the light of competition from the railways.

The railway came to Rye in 1851, after three years' wrangling between the London and Brighton, and the South Eastern, Railways, it being the latter that succeeded after some further three years in the construction; the Corporation supported the project by the necessary demolition of the almshouses, and the provision of a swing bridge over the Rother to accommodate shipping; the railway proved very popular, and the Rye Cattle Market Company purchased lands next to the station; in 1854, a branch line was constructed to serve Rye Harbour on the west side of the Rother, but although it never fulfilled commercial expectations, it remained open until 1960.

The golf course opened in 1894, and a popular 'steam tramline' was built to serve the club and the beach beyond; the line of the track is still visible near the Harbour Master's office, but it closed in 1939. The beach of Rye Bay became popular and, in the early twentieth century, Rye was a well-managed and largely self-sufficient town of substance; it was attractive to many literary figures, including Henry James who rented Lamb House, and who was followed by E. F. Benson.

The commercial traffic in the harbour increased into the mid twentieth century, but the further improvements of the 1960's were mostly to assist land drainage and the port activities lapsed into a final decline with the cessation of significant shipbuilding, but a new lifeboat station was built in 1966. The commercial use of the Town Quay is limited to about one movement a week, delivering Railtrack ballast, and a couple of small commercial quays upstream still maintain occasional activity. Today, Rye maintains an important inshore fishing fleet together with small-scale local industry, and is otherwise a tourist and sailing centre.

Around and About

It is impossible not to be enchanted by a day exploring the small town centre and, of all the Cinque Ports. The Heritage Information Centre off Strand Quay is a good starting point; there is a highly commendable range of publications available, and there is the beautifully prepared model of the medieval town with a recorded commentary lasting about a half-hour. Strand Quay was the principal trading area of the town, but few of the attractive timber clad buildings in the vicinity are of historical interest other than the northernmost, which was the Great Warehouse of 1736. At the eastern end of The Strand, as it turns into South Undercliff, there are narrow stone steps on the left leading up to the Hope Anchor Hotel in Watchbell Street, and there is the temptation to rest here; on the ascent, the nature of the sandstone cliff is apparent and, at the top, is the street from which warnings were given of French attacks.

The 'St Anthony'

In Watchbell Street, on the right, is the Catholic church of St Anthony of Padua, built to a fine standard in 1929. Nearby, are the *St Anthony*, a medieval merchant's house, and other fine properties including the old home of the Friars of the Sack, Stone House and the Methodist church, all in a delightful street scene. At the end, a short descent leads to the Gun Garden overlooking the old harbour, and off this is the welcoming Ypres Castle P.H. Above, is the Ypres Tower with its museum of local history, but opening times are limited.

The Ypres Castle P.H.

Regaining Watchbell Street, the churchyard of St Mary the Virgin is ahead, with its 1735 water cistern for the town supply. The church, dating from the mid twelfth century, is known as the cathedral of east Sussex and has been variously repaired and extended over the centuries; there is a wealth of interest within, and the climb to top of the tower is rewarded by a sight of the workings of the unique clock and magnificent views; it would be easy to spend an hour there.

Adjoining the church is Market Street and the traditional eighteenth century Town Hall that, at one time, had a market in the arcade below; within, is the roll of town mayors from 1289, and many interesting items including the two maces. At the top of East Street, a right turn leads into Hilders Cliff with superb views across the river. Hilders Cliff leads to the 1329 Landgate, still with its portcullis grooves, and from which the original town wall led westwards. A left turn from Landgate into Tower Street, and thence continuing into Cinque Ports Street, reveals lengths of the town walls behind the car park. A return along Cinque Ports Street enables an ascent up Conduit Hill, with the old municipal waterworks opposite, and thence to the High Street; near the corner is Adams of Rye, whose late eighteenth century property has a fine facade of mathematical tiling.

Within the High Street, notable buildings include Peacocke's 1636 Grammar School, and the sixteenth century George Hotel with its 1818 assembly room and minstrels' gallery, to say nothing of its comforts. Alongside the George Hotel is West Street, at the top corner of which is Lamb House, built in 1723 to a then leading design, and occupied by Henry James between 1897 and 1903; there are limited opening times to this National Trust property. Around the corner is the delightfully cobbled and steeply descending Mermaid Street.

The Mermaid Inn dates from the late fourteenth century, was rebuilt in the sixteenth, and it retains a wealth of period features; Jeake's House was built in 1690 as a wool warehouse, and the dwelling to the left was an early nineteenth century Quaker Meeting House. Hartshorn House is opposite; it was built in 1576 for a wealthy merchant, and it came into the Jeake's family at the end of the seventeenth century. At the foot of Mermaid Street are both The Mint and Wishward streets, lying behind Strand Quay.

Mermaid Street & the Mermaid Hotel

The half-hourly 'bus service for the couple of miles down to Rye Harbour provides a refreshing outing to this informal resort; there is the opportunity for a decent stroll beyond in a barely tamed environment alongside the river and down to the shingle beach.

It is difficult to become tired of Rye but, whilst all the above deserves better exploration, an opportunity to visit the *Antient Town* of Winchelsea should not be missed.

The thirty minutes' 'bus ride on Stagecoach route 711 provides the altogether differently rewarding experience. This, once important, small medieval 'new town' has an unusually spacious layout. There are the particular attractions of the church of St Thomas, the original Court Hall with its museum, other medieval buildings and splendid views across the countryside; the hospitality of both the Tea Rooms and the New Inn is excellent, but they are very busy in the tourist season.

Winchelsea: The Court House and Museum

Winchelsea: The Church of St Thomas

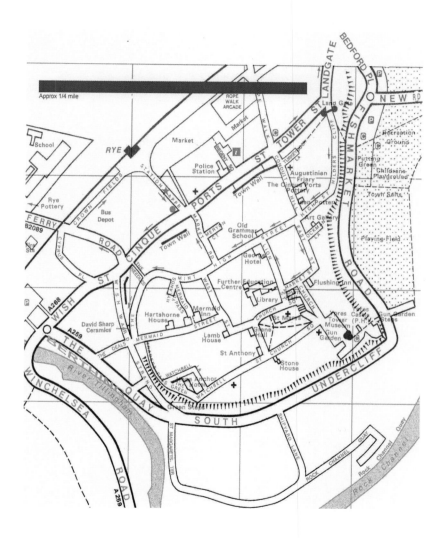

Rye Town Centre

Rail		Rye [1/2M] *[0845 748 4950]*
Buses		Stagecoach *[0870 608 2608]*
Taxis		Rother Cabs [224554]; Rye Motors [223176]
		Tollgate [230630]; Rye Motors [223176]
Hospital [A&E]		Conquest Hospital, Hastings *[01424 755 255]*
		The William Harvey, Ashford *[01233 633 331]*
Doctor		The Cinque Ports Surgery, Cinque Ports Street [223230]
		Postern Gate, Cinque Ports Street [223333]
Dentist [Private & NHS]		Messrs Davis & Seely, East Street [222834]
Police Station [not 24 hrs]		Cinque Ports Street *[0845 607 0999]*
Information Centre		The Heritage Information Centre, The Strand [226696]
		www.ryetourism.co.uk
Museum		Castle Museum, Ypres Tower, Castle Street
Churches	C of E	St Mary's, Market Street [222430]
	R C	St Anthony's, Watchbell Street [222173]
	Methodist	Church Square [223251]
Shops, Pharmacies and Banks		High Street
Supermarket		Budgens, Ferry Road
Public Houses		Numerous, of wide variety, but including
		The George Hotel [comfortable], High Street
		The Mermaid Inn [expensive, but must visit], Mermaid Street
		Ypres Castle Inn [beer garden], The Gun Garden
Restaurants		There are numerous cafes; among the more moderate restaurants are
		The George Hotel [very traditional], High Street [222114]
		Simply Italian [lively], The Strand [226024]
		The Lemon Grass [Thai], 1-2 Tower Street [222327]
		The Ypres Castle, Gun Garden [223248]
Entertainment		Leisure Centre, Love Lane
Town Events [subject to confirmation]		Charity Raft Race [August]
		Arts Festival [September]

Notes: Cooking aboard? Must visit the small fish shop in Rope Walk before 10.00hrs for the freshest selection of the local catch.

Approximate Tidal Difference -   Dover -0hrs20
Charts: Admiralty, 1991; Imray, 2100.5; Stanford, 9
Weather Forecasts   Harbour Office; Metcall [5 day] [09068 500 456]

Navigation Authority
            The Environment Agency, Worthing [01903 832 000] [0800 807060]
Coastguard   Dover [01304 210008]
Harbour Master   New Lydd Road, Camber [225225]
                                            Rye Harbour Radio Ch 14
Showers and Refuse   Strand Quay [Code from H.M.]

Fuel   Cans from garages; that in Winchelsea Road is the nearest to Strand Quay
                            Marine diesel from Rye Oil, Rye Harbour Road
                   [small quantities in cans, or 5,000l+ delivered] [223374]
              otherwise, apply to H.M. for access to the fishermen's common pool
Calor and Gaz   Sea Cruisers, Winchelsea Road

Berthing and Yards   Strand Quay [H.M.]
                     alongside tidal berthing; water, elec, showers, WC
                              Moon Marine, Rock Channel [222679]
                     tidal berthing between piles, but few short-term;
                     slip, general repairs, engineer, shower, WC
                                 River Brede Moorings [226213]
           tidal berthing between piles, but few short-term; general repairs
                 Other long-term tidal berths available; enquire of H.M.

Chandlers   Sea Cruisers, Winchelsea Road
Engineer, electronic   Sussex Fishing Services, 5 The Close [223895]
Sails and Rigging   Northrop Sails, Ramsgate [01843 851665]
                             Wilkinson Sails, Conyer, N. Kent [01795 521503]
Spars and Rigging   Southern Mast and Rigging, Brighton [01273 818189]

Notes: In the event of problems, the Harbour Master is there to assist

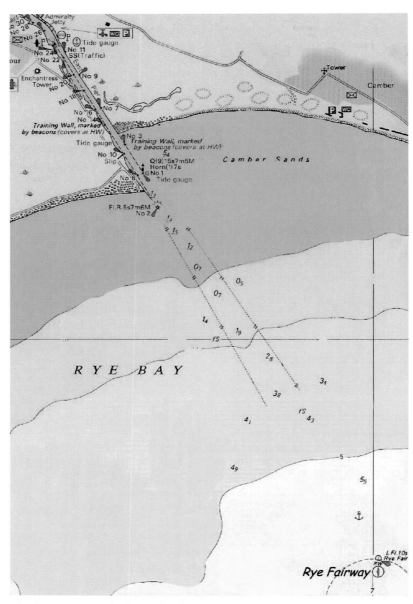

The Entrance to the River Rother   Adapted from Admiralty 1991

Navigation and Berthing

Tidal restrictions limit entrance to the harbour to between HW-2 and HW+3 but, without local knowledge, it should not be left later than HW+1; it is best to approach from a couple of miles off, and Rye Bay can be unpleasant in strong onshore winds; care should be taken also to avoid numerous anchored nets. Within this tidal range, the approach from the west presents no particular hazards once past the Royal Sovereign Shoals. The approach from the east requires avoidance of the Hythe and Lydd Firing Ranges when in use; they are then signalled by red flags and/or lights above the shoreline, and are monitored by a patrol boat; information as to firing times is available from the Rye Harbour Master's office [01797 225225], and Ch 73 or 13 should also be monitored.

The entrance can be made safely at night and under sail, given reasonable conditions. There is occasional commercial traffic, and the fishing fleet also; before making the final approach, it is sensible to check the level of activity with the Harbour Master [Rye Harbour Radio on Ch 14].

The inconspicuous entrance is guarded by a crescent of sandbanks just off, and these are always shifting. The approach should be made from *Rye Fairway* [RW. Lfl.10s] [$50^0$53.80N $00^0$48.13E], and then on a course of 329^0T for 1.8nM to leave the western breakwater No 2 mark [Fl. R.5.s] close to port, and this course continues upstream. The eastbound flood tide can make over 2kts across the entrance and the westbound a little less; within the channel, both flood and ebb can attain 5kts and this, combined with the cross tides, makes for unpredictable local currents; it is important therefore, to maintain the bearing.

The Entrance to the River Rother

With the western breakwater abeam, the eastern breakwater should be identified at some 240m upstream; this may be submerged at HW, but has a steel structure at its head with a green board above, illuminated at night [Q.(9)], and opposite this is No 6 light [Q.R]; the course remains at 329°T to pass midway between the two breakwaters, and is straight for about 0.7nM with the best water in the centre of the channel.

On the port hand, the western breakwater extends upstream into the Training Wall, a continuous structure which is submerged at HW, but which is marked by buoys [R., unlit] and withies, and which should be given a decent berth. Upstream, the Training Wall is continuous with the Town Quay and is not particularly obvious when submerged at HW springs. On the starboard hand, the eastern breakwater continues as a stone revetment, marked by lights [Fl.G.].

Once between the breakwaters, the harbour is well sheltered except from a strong southerly swell; from here, the visitor should proceed under engine within the speed limit of 6kts, and identify the Harbour Master's Office ahead at about 0.5nM on the starboard bank; this is the first substantial building on that hand, and comprises a modern two-storey structure with radio mast behind. If VHF contact has not already been made, it is now appropriate to do so to confirm the absence of commercial traffic; above the office are IPT Signals [RRR, GGG] which, if switched on, must meet with compliance, even if that entails stemming the tide and tucking tightly inshore. The commercial traffic comprises the occasional 25m coaster, and there is also an active fishing fleet; there is room to pass, but with little margin and a lookout astern should be maintained.

The Harbour Master's Office

The Harbour Office is open during normal working hours, seven days a week, and at other times when there is commercial traffic. Unless prior arrangements have been made, visitors are required to report on arrival; timber staging immediately upstream of the Office has been provided for this purpose, and arrival near slack water is much the easiest.

The Office will give berthing directions, collect harbour dues and berthing fees, and issue the useful 'Mariners' Guide to Rye' together with a copy of the harbour bye-laws and the security code to the WC/shower. Arrivals out of hours may proceed directly to their berth, but must report in the next morning; however, it is unwise for night arrivals to proceed further in the absence of local knowledge, and should be prepared to take to the ground at the additional staging immediately upstream.

The choice of berthing at Rye is limited. The staging upstream of the Office has WC/shower facilities nearby [code from Harbour Office]; it is useful to those, including fishing vessels, who wish to take an early morning tide, but this is an isolated outpost a couple of miles from the town, and the river bed alongside dries to a hard bottom.

On the west bank opposite, is the village of Rye Harbour with dinghy sailing club, PH, café, and the Lifeboat Station; moorings here are mostly for small craft, and there is no allocation for visitors; the Town Quay there is covered at HW springs, and is available only for a short stay. There are numerous small yards and lengths of private moorings upstream and in Rock Channel, but these do not cater for the casual visitor; there are usually some longer-term tidal berths available, but these are best reconnoitred from the land as conditions vary widely.

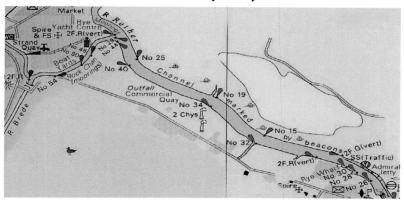

The Rother & Rock Channel [not to scale]

The visitors' moorings are situated principally therefore at Strand Quay, and the approach is *via* Rock Channel. At 1nM upstream from the Harbour Office, the uninspiring entrance to the Channel will be found on the port hand, and is marked by the buoys Nos *44* [QR] and *29* [QG]; the turn is tight, but identification is assisted by a large sign and arrow on the Channel's s'board bank. If the turning is missed, the continuation upstream leads past another couple of small yards and the fishing fleet; beyond, is the road bridge with an air draft of less than 3m.

Rock Channel is well buoyed and runs reasonably true past stretches of unattractive mud berths for about 0.3nM to an obvious bend to s'board and a small basin to be ignored, before a gentle bend to port at the commencement of Strand Quay. There is a welcoming notice on the s'board hand immediately past a public slipway. Visitors are expected to berth on the town side [s'board hand on approach], and there is adequate space for turning.

The Uninspiring Entrance to Rock Channel at Low Water

Strand Quay at Low Water
[and out of season]

The Quay is about 200m in length, of steel piled walling with fixed ladders every 15m, together with timber whalings and rings for mast strops, but fender boards are not provided. The channel here dries to a trickle at about chart datum, with the best water towards the downstream end; berthing is on soft clean mud, the banks of which rise 1.5m or so above the channel, and mast strops are recommended for the first tide; a little thought is necessary to make best use of the spacing between the ladders and the power supply boxes, but rafting up is not encouraged. Long bow and stern lines are required to accommodate the rise and fall of around 3m, and fender boards should be watched for snagging.

The Quay can become crowded in season, and attracts visitors from 'across the water'; it is better to arrive early rather than late, notwithstanding having had to back the tide on reporting at the Harbour Master's office. The WC/shower [free of charge] is nearby in a single, modern and comfortably sized family unit, adjoining the public conveniences; the coffee shops profit from the inevitable waiting time, and a crewmember needs to be posted as a lookout! The ambience is uniquely pleasant; berthing at the downstream end minimises nuisance from traffic noise and street lighting. The seagulls are dire if attracted by titbits.

Dover Castle from the Town

The town is tensed between the brooding presence of the Castle and the busy port below. Whilst complementary in historical function, they nevertheless leave the town with a weak sense of identity.

DOVER

DOVER is port and castle at England's 'Gateway to Europe' and, in this sense, it has remained unchanged since the Bronze Age; indeed, here is the earliest excavated sea-going boat in the world. The town is one of contrasts between its efficient port, marina and outstanding attractions, and a hillside town centre whose potential charm has been abandoned to appalling piecemeal development. The yachtsman entering this busy port in a professional manner is met with helpful courtesy; a full day's stopover is inadequate to take on board the principal attractions, but the town centre is a good half-mile from the marina.

History

The earliest evidence of Dover's history dates from the Iron Age earthwork defences, and subsequently those of the Bronze Age; they were sufficient to deter the Romans from landing at the Dour Valley, but fell eventually. The Roman *pharos*, or lighthouse, still stands in the Castle grounds; it was constructed from local 'tufa' stone, reinforced with tiles and, although the uppermost two storeys have disappeared, it is a monument to Roman building quality; another *pharos* on the western heights is no more. The port was the base for the Roman navy; in the town is the Roman 'Painted House' which was built as an hotel for visiting dignitaries, and which is also the site of an early Roman defensive shore fort. At that time, the marshy haven ran back between the hills at least as far as what is now the Market Square; it was never large, but simply one which coincided with the shortest sea crossing from mainland Europe and, of all the ports under the command of the Count of the Saxon Shore, it was the only one to become a Cinque Port.

In spite of the port's limitations, its importance continued to grow after the Roman withdrawal. The town was granted burgh status in about 830 and, in return for rights of self-government, fishing, and continental trading, it was made responsible for its own defences; indeed, under King Edward the Elder at end of the ninth century, it had its own mint. It seems however that there may have been two burghs, one on the west side of the Dour Valley, and the other around the Castle Hill; on the latter, there still stands the main Saxon church of St Mary-in-Castro, abutting the *pharos*, and built on an earlier structure at the instigation of King Harold; nearby, is the chapel consecrated in 1253 by St Richard of Chichester in honour of

St Edmund. There has hardly been a subsequent era in which the fortifica-
tions have not been extended or modified, even to the neglect of the other
Ports, and the Castle today is a magnificent standing commentary on
English history to the mid-twentieth century.

There is little subsequent history of note until the twelfth century,
when Godwin, as Earl of Kent, is thought generally to have well looked
after the people of Dover. In 1051 there was the unfortunate visit there by
Count Eustace of Bordeaux on his way to London; evidently, Eustace
expected a greater degree of subservient hospitality than was forthcoming,
and it was Godwin's insistence on a fair trial for the men of the town that
led to his confrontation with the king.

In those times, Dover was little scathed by the Danish attacks, and
was defended strongly enough to deter William of Normandy from landing
there; instead, he took it from the rear. There is conflicting evidence as to
whether the Castle surrendered or was taken, but probably the latter as
William had the defenders Ashburton and his son beheaded at the gate at the
top of the hill, and he expelled the civilian population prior to installing his
own garrison; following this, his men went on the rampage and sacked the
town. William recognised the importance of restoring the town's goodwill,
and it was hence one of the few which received proper compensation for the
damage done; he then re-affirmed the town's privileges, and initiated a great
rebuilding programme which was to continue into the thirteenth century,
creating a virtually new town. This recognition of the town's status was
rewarded in 1069 by the Dover ships defeating a large Danish raiding party,
and again in their support for the Scottish expedition of 1091 in which many
of their ships and crew were lost.

With considerable and justifiable misgivings, William appointed
his half-brother Odo, the Bishop of Bayeux, as practical successor to
Godwin. As the new Earl of Kent and Lord of Dover Castle, he chose Hugh
de Montfort as Constable; he also grew over-ambitious and was called to
account by Archbishop Langfranc for encroachment on church estates, that
were recovered as a result. His unpopularity even caused a popular uprising
that drove the locals to making peace with Eustace; the result was a poorly
executed raid on the castle, and a further and equally unsuccessful support-
ive raid by the Danes. William imprisoned Odo and stripped him of his
position before exiling him, but the constableship of the castle remained
with de Montfort.

The Domesday Book describes Dover as a settlement to the west
of the present Market Square, and the land under the cliff between old St
James church and the sea, together with the old borough on Castle Hill
where the size St Mary in Castro is indicative of a substantial community
having developed there; this must have been an awkward sprawl, with the
two shore level communities separated by the Dour's estuarial marshes. The

early buildings in the town were extensive; they included the Guildhall, the church of St Peter in Market Square, the old church of St James, a small hospice for travellers which developed substantially and eventually became the Town Hall, the church of St Mary the Virgin which grew from its original two-cell structure to its present size, and a further group of houses at Warden Down. Another major building was the church of St Martin le Grand for the 'secular canons', and which covered the site of the old shore fort; there were running disputes between the church and canons over whom it had no authority; eventually, Henry I was persuaded to permit a new monastery for the regular canons, and to transfer all assets of St Martin le Grand to the new. Originally, the new was named St Martin of New Wark, but it came to be known as Dover Priory; it was demolished in the nineteenth century, and Dover College now stands on its site. It was therefore Richard, as the Prior of St Martins, who was elected Primate in 1174 following the murder of Thomas A'Beckett.

At the time of Domesday the town was managed by a 'praeposter', a position later to become that of the mayor, together with a reeve and burgesses; one praeposter, William Godfrey, is recorded as owning two houses and the Guildhall. The municipal arrangements were more advanced than in many other towns, reflecting the already considerable cross channel trade, with well-established packet-boat services including that with Wissant - a harbour which has long disappeared; the town was divided into twenty-one wards, each of which had the right to run one packet boat in return for its ship service. '... whenever the King's messengers came there, they paid three pence for the passage of a horse in the winter and two pence in the summer, the burgesses finding a steersman and one other helper'. There was not only the packet-boat service, but also the port's own pilot service until 1853, when it was merged with that of Trinity House.

On the death of Henry I in 1135, King Stephen found Canterbury and Dover held for the Empress Maud by her half brother Richard of Gloucester; whilst he submitted within a year, Dover Castle under Walkelin Marminot, did not until it fell to a blockade by her ships from Boulogne. It was Henry II however, who replaced with stonework the early earthworks and their timber palisades on the hill; this work commenced in 1180 under the supervision of Master Ralph and Maurice the Engineer, to provide the great Keep and the bailey walls; these were incomplete at the time of his death, and were continued in the time of King Richard I. The resulting Keep, of about 30m square, is of massive construction and is possibly the best in England; its entrance is at second floor level, just inside which is a 100m fresh water well, and there are still traces of the sophisticated lead distribution pipework; on the same level within the Keep's 6m thick walls are the two great apartments, with stairways leading to numerous other rooms, and to the roof from which there are superb views; the Palace Gate on the south side, and the King's Gate on the north, are also from this period.

The Port's fleet had taken the major part in the transport for the capture of Lisbon from the Moors in 1147, and then provided much of that for Richard I's crusading army of 1190. It was in about 1200 that John reinforced the outer wall and gates of the Castle, and appointed Hugo de Burgh as Constable over its complement of ten knights supported by their men-at-arms; de Burgh promptly proceeded to undertake extensive underground works to provide a series of tunnels, for a combination of storage and facilitating troop movement. This was one of John's better appointments, for he also founded the Maison Dieu in 1203 as a hostel for the many impecunious pilgrims travelling to and from the continent, and later it accommodated sick and wounded soldiers returning from the continent. In 1224, the work of Christianising England was continued by the arrival at Dover of the Friars Preachers, otherwise known as the Black Friars or Dominicans.

At this time, England was under constant attack from the French under Louis the son of the French king and, following the loss of Normandy, the Dover fleet was frequently called for beyond their 15 days' service. In 1213, at the Battle of Damme, hundreds of French ships were sunk or captured, but the hopes that this would discourage the French were disappointed. John, facing ever-increasing pressures from both the barons at home and from his continental enemies, was, for a time, forced to take refuge in the Castle; it was from here that he sought an unsuccessful respite by endeavouring to hand the country over to the Papal States.

In 1216, Louis' army landed at Rye, occupied much of Kent around Canterbury, took Rochester and entered London, all whilst John's countermeasures were conspicuously incompetent, and leaving Dover as the country's last bastion under Hubert de Burgh; the besieged castle was saved by a force of four hundred men under Simon de Pencestre, who entered by secret tunnels notwithstanding the near-successful French attempts at mining an entrance. It was from here that de Burgh as Admiral of the Cinque Ports' fleet, set out to defeat the French at the Battle of Sandwich in 1216, thus ending French territorial aspirations for the immediate future.

In 1217 however, another French army sailed for London in a fleet of 86 cogs under the command of Eustace the Monk, who had at one time been commander of one of the Cinque Ports' fleets. A fleet of 16 well-armed large, and some 20 smaller, Dover vessels attacked from astern and downwind, grappled, and threw quicklime into the enemy's faces, followed by volleys of arrows, before boarding and cutting away the rigging; although the French long complained at foul play, this was merely an extension of quite orthodox tactics.

It was in about that year that de Burgh resigned the management of the *Maison Dieu* to the new King Henry III; the House had been used from time to time by John to make his proclamations to the Ports, and this practice was followed by subsequent kings; in 1227, Henry III dedicated it to the Blessed Virgin Mary. The House seems largely to have been sustained by numerous small payments in kind; its records include that of one *'William Burmashe and his brethren* [who gave] *ninety-five pence, twenty-four hens and one hundred eggs'*.

The outer wall of the castle was erected in the mid thirteenth century; there are various towers, including watch towers and the Constable's Gate, and the latter is the main entrance and residence of the Commanding Officer; the debtors' prison near Canon Gate was originally the general prison for the Cinque Ports, and was only closed in 1855, but not demolished until 1911. Hubert de Burgh held office as Lord Warden between 1202 and 1232, except for short periods when other appointments were made, including that of William de Longspee. In 1258, for the better administration of defence, the offices of Lord Warden and Constable were combined. In the Wars of the barons, Sir Roger de Leybourne seized the castle and port to prevent the French mercenaries from landing and assisting the king but Simon de Montfort took it in his absence and Sir Roger was then held there.

Simon de Pencestre held office from 1265 to 1298, and brought a degree of organisation to the previously vague administration of the Castle and the Cinque Ports; he drew up the Statutes of Dover Castle, concerning religious observance, and punishments for falling asleep whilst on watch and for foul language; the defensive duties included regulating the watches and closing the gates at night and, on one occasion, even the king himself was unable to gain entry. It was during his tenure that there were rumours of a combined Irish and French force assisting the William of Orange; these rumours were unfounded, but nevertheless some 300 townspeople assembled and took over the castle, as a result of which it was thereafter garrisoned.

In the Barons' War of 1258-1265, Dover was clearly on the side of Simon de Montfort, but nevertheless later supported Edward's Welsh campaign of 1282, losing many ships and men in the capture of Anglesey; it had recovered sufficiently by 1290, to support the extended Scottish campaign, but the French were becoming a major threat with their larger ships and improved seamanship. In 1295 the French fleet attacked, but were driven off. They attacked again, unexpectedly on the western side, and put ashore perhaps fifteen thousand men and set about burning the town; many of the inhabitants fled, and it was left to neighbouring communities to assemble and drive them off with great losses; Thomas de Hale, the prior of Dover Priory, resisted the surrender of church plate, and was killed. The damage to the town was compounded by a large cliff fall that completely blocked the harbour and, in the year of the sacking, the port could find no more than seven ships; some five years later, it could still find only eight and, in 1297 it petitioned to be allowed to hire a ship for fulfillment of its ship service.

The town made slow recovery, but remained the embarkation point for numerous noteworthy passages. In 1308, the Prince Regent, later Edward II, departed from there for his marriage with Isabella of Spain, and this was an occasion of great pageantry which must have relieved the townsfolk's otherwise grim lifestyle. From this period, Dover became a flourishing port for trade and the transport of armies and pilgrims, and it maintained its small-scale shipbuilding off the beach. The volume of traffic grew to the extent that it became a matter of national security; Edward I made several regulations for the transport service, including the status of the Cinque Ports' Pilots. It was his charter that not only regulated the tariffs for the crossing, but also laid down the allocation of boats and passengers for the benefit of the poorer pilgrims, and these regulations lasted until the time of King Henry VIII; there also came about the requirement for all persons leaving the country to embark at a stated port, and Dover was the one selected in 1336. Dover's fleet however, was never one of the largest; for the siege of Calais in 1347, it sent sixteen ships, against the twenty-two of Sandwich and the twenty-one of Winchelsea, but these were only of the 735 impressed total.

By the mid fourteenth century, the town was again in decline. The increasing threat from the French caused the building of the town wall and its gates from 1368, and they were completed by 1384; the money for these works was raised as the work proceeded, by a local tax known as the 'cess'. This drain on the town's resources was exacerbated by the Dour estuary becoming choked and, even worse, was the sea breaching the town wall.

It was the Castle's strategic location which saved it from obsolescence in the face of the introduction of effective siege cannons and, when King Henry III ascended the throne to settle the country, he set to repairing the castle and improving the fortifications; he had blocked up the vulnerable north gate with high ground outside, and had St John's tower built outside the gate; access to the castle was provided by a small opening in the outer walls, known as Constable's Tower; this remains in use as the official office of the Lord Warden. The defences were insufficient for the town to resist the French in 1337; the castle was held, but the town was plundered, the priory similarly so for its plate, and the town's charters were carried off. In 1340 however, the Dover fleet was involved in the Battle of Sluys and, in 1346, in transport for the Battle of Crecy. The fleet served again in 1415 in transport for Agincourt, and afterwards there was a magnificent victory procession through the town led by Henry V; his body was brought to Dover after his death in 1422, and was again the occasion for a procession although of a necessarily sombre nature. These invaluable services were costly to the town and, in 1424, a Mandate annexed Margate, Ringwould, Kingsdown, St Johns, St Peters, Goresend and Birchington as non-corporate Members.

In the Wars of the Roses the Dover people together with most of the other Portsmen 'favoured the white', probably following the example of the Earl of Warwick. King Edward IV revenged himself by seizing the liberties of the town in 1469, and for a while imposed a royal custodian; by then, and as mentioned in his charter, Dover was in a miserable state; it nevertheless received his favour in 1473, when he gave a ten years' grant to repair the storm-damaged town walling; indeed the charter of Henry VI stated that the town was ruined by numerous inundations, notwithstanding Edward's £10,000 expenditure on the Keep alone.

The harbour has a history of problems. The sea had been receding from Saxon times but, by the fourteenth century, it began re-encroaching and threatening the buildings in Market Place; a retaining wall known as the 'Old Wyke' was built together with a new quay and promenade behind, to create an inlet below the old St James's church, and a little cove on the western side was improved where the shipbuilding yards were located. Dover and Sandwich were in competition, and it was Dover that took the opportunity to build a new harbour; in 1474 and 1481, the king granted tolls to enable repairs, as it was no longer possible to maintain shelter and wharfage on the eastern side of the bay; as recorded in Hollingshed's Chronicle, *"There was a round tower built by one John Clarke, Priest, Master of the Maison Dieu, about the year 1500, at the south-west side of the Bay, which served somewhat to defend ships from the rage of the south-west winds, but especially to moor ships that were tied thereto. Many great rings were fastened to the tower for that purpose'.* Its value was reflected in the name given to it of 'Paradise' but a combination of gales and the eastwards drift of shingle partly destroyed it in 1530, and it was not until the 1580s that further works were undertaken.

King Henry VIII again recognised the town's strategic importance. The Castle was not adapted as a gun platform, but a number of small blockhouse batteries were constructed at the foot of the cliffs. He built two small shore defence castles, as well as the harbour mole with two towers at the end; the harbour works alone cost £68,000, although the sea damaged most of them. It was partly through his direct intervention that the court of lodemanage was established, to avoid the admiralty court of Dover being concerned with the continuing minor disputes among the pilots; this court sat under a panel of *'four respectable mariners',* but its powers grew sufficiently to cause complaint, and the Lord Warden had to impose further control; this court continued until the Dover pilots were merged with those of Trinity House.

Dover was Henry's point of departure for his meeting at the 'Field of the Cloth of Gold' in France with Francois I in 1520, and transported by a fleet from the Cinque Ports; his retinue was vast, and it was accompanied by Thomas Wolseley, the Cardinal of York, by Charles, the Duke of Suffolk, and by many others. The town was still in poor condition, and the harbour was badly silted; the demand for fish had dropped as the religious houses were in decline; the Priory was practically insolvent, and there were few canons remaining; St Martin le Grand was beyond economic repair.

His wanton asset stripping at the time of the Reformation included the ending of the Maison Dieu as an institution. The early parish church of St Mary the Virgin, in Biggin Street however, at least had his formal recognition, and it remains of particular interest; the tower has had a clock since 1539, but the present clock is nineteenth century, and there is a seventeenth century sundial on the south side. In the time of Charles II, the Mayor, Corporation and Jurats occupied seats behind the altar and, notwithstanding objections, this *'indecent practice of sitting round the Altar'* was continued until 1836; it was also within this church, that the freemen of the town elected their mayor. The Pilots of the Cinque Ports erected their own gallery there in 1698, and it was moved to its present position in 1843 when the church was largely rebuilt; the merger of the Ports' Pilots with those Trinity House is recalled by the coat of arms of the Master and Brethren of Trinity House, Deptford Strond, displayed on the front of the gallery.

Henry had left himself open to attack from the combined forces of the Papal, French and Spanish states. Dover, of course, already had its castle, but three small castles and gun emplacements were added to cover the beaches; the old 'Black Battery' is now covered by the Western Docks. He also supported the construction of the great western breakwater, the placement of the stones for which was the Archimedes principle was used in carrying them underwater; this work was never finished, and the great storm of 1539 deposited such huge quantities of shingle that the harbour was completely closed.

It was Mary Tudor who further fortified the castle with the tower now named after her; she also took pains to restore the harbour, and her letter to the bailiffs and jurats is still preserved as a testimony to her efforts.

Justice of the day in the town was salutary. In the first year of her reign, one Richard Shooder being found guilty of being a common cut-purse, was sentenced to be pinned by his ear to the pillory, and to remain there until he had cut himself free with the knife left beside him; thereafter, anyone found earless in the town was condemned to death; court records indicate that capital punishment comprised being thrown over Sharpness

Cliff, with the added twist that it was the accuser who was required to carry out the punishment.

The town was not in itself of great importance because, according to Queen Elizabeth, there were no more than 358 houses of which 9 were uninhabited; its *'shippers and crayers'* numbered only 20 of *'small burthen'* whilst there were only 130 persons engaged in *'marchard and fyshing'*; these numbers probably related only to the freemen or those in authority. By this time, nothing remained of the original harbour; it was saved by the discovery of a high level spring above, and which was dammed to form a pent for periodic scouring, the cost of which was met by a charter for *'Rivage and Feriage'* enabling the town to license boats for landing and to charge dues for bringing people and baggage ashore. In response to a later petition penned by Sir Walter Raleigh, Elizabeth visited the town, notwithstanding the people of Folkestone trying to *'divert her favours to themselves'*; she remained six days in the castle and, as a result of her visit, the town was granted the free exportation of *'3000 qtrs of wheat, 10000 of barley or malt, and 10000 tuns of beer'*. This patent was sold for the sum of £8,666.13s.4d., and the money was directed to both castle and harbour, but the works ran out of funds by 1582 as a result of poor planning, with little to show for their efforts.

The castle's condition deteriorated after an earthquake in 1580, but a further application to the queen resulted in a grant of *'threepence in the ton on every vessel loading or unloading in any port within the realm for seven years'*; the works to the castle and harbour continued for some years, and the present harbour dates from those times. The queen was rewarded at the time of the Armada by the town providing the *Elizabeth* of 120 tons with a crew of 120 and provisions for 50 days; it was this ship which decoyed the Spanish *Galleas* onto the beach at Calais, where she was burned. The town supplied several other smaller vessels, including the fire ships that in the event were not used.

Whilst Elizabeth had given the town an elective mayor, and James I between 1603 and 1610 had granted 'passing tolls' which were applied to improving the pent, he regarded the harbour as mismanaged. In 1606, he seized control and imposed his own board comprising the Lord Warden and seven assistants, all non-resident in Dover; the members had little expertise and, although its constitution continued to the twentieth century, in its early days it did little for the advancement of the harbour; this had changed by the twentieth century, by which time it comprised the Lord Warden, two Dover barons, two government and two railway nominees.

In 1625 Charles I came to meet his bride, Henrietta Maria; he spent £2,600 on the apartments at the castle, but nothing on its defence or on the harbour. The castle had been held for the king at the time of the Great Rebellion in 1642, but was taken with ease by a handful of the parliamentary force, and the town remained loyal to that cause in spite of some disturbances until the restoration of the monarchy. As with many towns, a 'return of suspects' was made of those who had been carefully watched; thus, one return made by Mr. Reynolds the Registrar for Dover includes *'Dover: Arnold Braems, merchant. 6ᵗʰ Feb. 1656, at the house of Mr. Richard Harrison, a tailor over against the Dolphin Tavern, in Tower Street, in the Parish of Barking. 12ᵗʰ Feb. Braines gives notice of removal to Dover. 12ᵗʰ March. Againe at Harrison's. 19ᵗʰ May. Arnold Braems of Bridge went to the house of Harrison, a tayler, etc.'* In 1650, the plague had reached Dover, brought by a servant from London, and hundreds were buried in 'The Graves' north of Archcliff Fort.

In 1660, King Charles II returned in triumph from his exile. He had sailed from Sluys in the *Naseby* under the command of Captain William Stokes, a Dover man, together with a fleet of twenty-six vessels, and among the many personages who accompanied him was the diarist Pepys; he arrived in Dover at two o'clock in the afternoon, but suffered the indignity of being rowed ashore due to the silting of the harbour. There was a magnificent reception, at which he was welcomed by the Lord General Monk, the Earl of Winchelsea, and the Constable of Dover Castle, together with the Mayor of Dover and his corporation; the king responded by presenting the mayor with a silver mace and, shortly afterwards £30,000 to be spent on the repair of the harbour, and he reinstated the passing tolls subject to supervision by Trinity House; the Paradise was abandoned, and the harbour extended by blocking the bottom of the pent itself. He also displayed his displeasure at the town having supported the Parliamentarians, by withdrawing Elizabeth's charter, and granting his own; he thenceforth frequently interfered in the town's affairs and choice of leaders, including throwing some out of office, and appointing his victualling officer in Maison Dieu House; this was built in 1665 adjoining the Maison Dieu itself, in the year that the plague struck again with over 900 deaths. By then, the castle was severely dilapidated, and Paradise was merely marshland; this was subsequently reclaimed, and over it now runs Limekiln Street.

Charles appointed his brother James, later King James II, as Lord Warden; in 1668, he was installed at the Bredenstone on the Western Heights in accordance with tradition and, in 1989, there was a public celebration in Market Square to celebrate his flight from the country. He had done nothing for the town and, by 1676, it was necessary to revive an ancient custom of beating the drum to call out every burgess to shovel away the shingle from the harbour. In 1689, the harbour was again in disrepair, and the town petitioned for it to be made good, alleging that merchantmen valued at £140,000 had recently taken refuge there from either or both of storms and the French, and that more would have been saved but for the shallows at its entrance; by 1699, the entrance was impassable, even for the packet boats.

During reign of Queen Anne, around 2,000 French prisoners were held in the castle, but with little supervision; as a result, they ransacked the place, tearing up flooring and panelling for firewood; the castle from thenceforth seems to have been held in little esteem, and was allowed to fall into disrepair, and the harbour equally so. The town was an unplanned agglomeration of mostly poor buildings with a central drainage ditch exiting into the harbour; unsurprisingly, there were frequent house fires, and disease was endemic. It was a tight and introverted community, into which strangers were neither welcomed, nor permitted to take up employment, nor to start their own business.

There was some improvement effected in 1700 and 1718; in 1714, the Duke of Marlborough had landed there, not knowing that Queen Anne had died that day. In 1723, two-thirds of the passing tolls were allocated to Rye, leaving Dover to continue with the laborious process of hand-clearing the shingle. The engineer Smeaton, famous for his design of the Eddystone lighthouse, was appointed to report on the harbour in 1769, but his simple recommendations were ignored. Work to the harbour recommenced in 1782 to better effect with the construction of the Admiralty Pier, and with the Wellington and Granville Docks taking much of their present form; there was now the facility for berthing ships of up to 800 tons, as well as the new and faster packet boats, but there remained the problem of shingle build-up. A further report by the engineer Nickalls in 1783 was also largely ignored and, by 1791, the harbour was again in a poor state.

It had been the substantial increase in trade and travel of the mid eighteenth century, notwithstanding the sporadic wars, which had prompted attention to the harbour; the new turnpike roads were under construction, with those between Dover and Folkestone, and Dover and Barham, completed in 1753, that between Deal and Sandwich in 1797, and others by 1801. The strategic importance of the port and castle had also become sufficiently obvious during the Napoleonic Wars; there was a detailed survey of the castle, as even the additional batteries which had been constructed in 1779 had fallen into decay; at an immediate expenditure of £50,000, it was provided with additional batteries and better gun positions, extensions to the tunnels, and further improvements to accommodate 1000 troops, but at the sacrifice of some of the older parts. Almost simultaneously, the major defensive works on the Western Heights were undertaken, including the unique triple spiral stairway to enable rapid deployment; on these heights are the remains of the nineteenth century excavations of a church once attributed to the Knights Templars, and it was one of the old meeting places of the court of Shepway.

In 1808 however, the sea breached the North Pier, and this was repaired in the shadow of yet more wrangling over the necessary major improvements, with financial restrictions at every stage. The Admiralty later decided to proceed with works to the Admiralty Pier and, by 1850, it had been lengthened to 4,000ft; it was carried out into the tideway, thus providing a permanent solution to the building up of the shingle bar at the entrance. It was from this improved harbour that the exiled Louis XVIII returned to France in 1814 with much ceremony; in the same year, the Czar arrived and left, followed by the arrival of the injured Queen Caroline in 1820, which coincided with the year of the first steam packet, the *Rob Roy*.

There were great municipal changes between 1778-1835, reflecting the town's new society, largely brought about by the garrisoning of troops there; these changes included the provision of street lighting and the regulation of bathing. Dover became almost fashionable, with Marine Parade built in 1820, the Esplanade in 1833, and Waterloo Crescent in 1834; these were about the only parts of significance to survive the 1939-1945 war, probably because of their landmarks' value to enemy aircraft. The Southeastern Railway arrived in 1844, the London, Chatham and Dover Railway in 1860 and the direct line to London via Canterbury in 1861. The railway line was extended to the western docks, which was already a cruise terminal; the Lord Warden Hotel was built there, and remained in use as such until 1939, when it became used for offices. In 1861, there was the development of the sea-front, and development on the old shingle bank ropewalk; in the same year, the Harbour Board was overhauled and new appointments made in response to continuing complaints at the old; in the same year, the passing tolls were at last abolished. In 1897, there was the first electric tramway in the town, but it was not until 1937 that it was replaced with 'buses. Dover was Captain Webb's point of departure for the first cross-channel swim in 1875, it was the landing place of the first cross-channel flight by Bleriot in 1909, and is marked by a white outline in the grass near the Castle; in the next year, Stewart Rolls made the first cross-channel return flight.

The Admiralty continued its improvements, independently of the harbour Board, to provide a harbour of refuge for twenty battleships, but this was not opened until 1907. In the 1914-1918 war, Dover became a naval port, and was the headquarters of the Dover Patrol; initially, the Patrol was largely of impressed ships manned by fishermen, tugmen and lightermen, together with a few senior officers from the RNVR. At the commencement of the 1939-1945 war, all civilian cross-channel traffic was diverted to Folkestone; the Civil Defence was organised by the Chief Constable of Dover Castle and the Mayor, and shelters were provided in the caves in the cliff face. The harbour, although of limited value due to its exposure to the long-range guns, was vital to the resurrected Dover Patrol operating primarily as minesweepers and minelayers, and also as rescue ships. The Castle was guarded by six gun batteries, the tunnels beneath were again extended, and it was the command post for the evacuation of Dunkirk; the 'Little Ships' of that operation were those commandeered from the creeks and harbours of the Cinque Ports.

The modern history of Dover is again centred on the docks and their cross-channel trade. The expansion of post-war leisure travel prompted the expansion of the Eastern Docks, and the removal of much of the commercial traffic to the Western, with the now redundant Hovercraft terminal used by the Hoverspeed Fast Ferry; all this has resulted in the singularly unattractive road improvements in the area of Snargate and Townwall Street. A stroll into the Western Docks, and onto the Pier overlooking the present cruise terminal, is a hunting ground for those interested in commercial archaeology.

Around and About

A day spent at Dover castle in reasonable weather will be an amazing experience, although in season the mid-week is far better than the weekends; the 'bus stop is at the bottom of the hill, so the better option is to take a taxi from the marina towards the Canon's Gateway and avoid the long uphill hike; a picnic is well worth considering, although the catering facilities there are surprisingly good. The Castle attractions are manifold, and useful information sheets are available on site.

The Roman *Pharos* and St Mary in Castro

The complexity of its history results in ever more being discovered, and opened to the public in a highly professional manner. It is best to commence early with the Secret Wartime Tunnels because of queuing, and the guided tour takes about an hour. At the Keep Yard, there is an introductory twelve minutes' film and an hour's presentation; the Keep itself almost beggars belief, and a couple of hours can pass quickly, especially if the towers are climbed and the views savoured.

There are the medieval tunnels, for which there is a three quarter hour's guided tour, numerous exhibitions, and a free circulating road-train. There is also a circuitous walk around the battlements and gateways, and much open space around the *Pharos* and the church of St Mary in Castro; the site extends to a total of about 12 acres with outstanding picnic sites. The mile walk from the Constable's Tower back down Castle Hill Road leads past the old St James's church in St James' Street, sadly ruined by bomb damage but still substantial; the side chapel was used as a courtroom by the Cinque Ports' barons and by the Lodemanage, and as the meeting place of the Shepway until 1851. To the immediate east, are the ruins of Henry VIII's Moat Bulwark and the East Cliff fortifications; from there, it is another mile back to the marina.

The Church of St James

There is, for the energetic, a further two miles' walk along the cliff tops to the old North Foreland lighthouse [open from 11.00hrs to 17.00hrs Thursdays to Mondays, March to October, and every day June to August]; refreshments are available. The adjoining areas of chalk downland provide a rare habitat for many species of plants and insects.

Dover Town Centre

Although Dover's town centre is unattractive, it nevertheless includes many locations of interest. To the east of the marina, is the vaunted de Bradelei Wharf shopping centre of 'factory outlets', but this is little different from those attaching themselves to many other marinas. Behind, there is the fine Marine Parade and Waterloo Crescent with the Royal Cinque Ports Yacht Club; the club is poorly supported, but has a good terrace overlooking the harbour.

The pedestrian underpass to the town centre was the site of the discovered Bronze Age boat; it leads into the bottom of Cannon Street, and thence to Market Square; to the left of the Square, is the Dover Museum and Bronze Age Boat Gallery. A little further up, Cannon Street becomes Biggin Street; on the right, is the church of St Mary the Virgin, and the last shell to be fired from France to Dover in 1944 landed nearby; the Pencester Gardens and the trickle of the River Dour are behind the church. The entrance to the Roman Painted House in Biggin Street is almost opposite the church, and is reputedly the best preserved in southern England; it contains much of the original hypocaust, together with outstanding wall decorations.

The *Maison Dieu* and Maison Dieu House

A little further up Biggin Street is the *Maison Dieu*; it was purchased and restored by the Corporation in 1834, and now houses a collection of portraits of the Lord Wardens, the original banner of the Ports carried to the Yarmouth Fair, and a somewhat eclectic display of armoury, but opening times are erratic. The Information Centre is at the side and, adjacent, is the Maison Dieu House with the Public Library.

Waterloo Crescent and the Beach

     The Western Heights are an unique defensive complex, comple-
menting the Castle; they were designed primarily to prevent the town being
taken from the rear, and comprise a wide and extensive variety of fortifications from the Napoleonic era. All are set within what is now a nature
reserve, and some of the views are more interesting than those from the
Castle. Access from the town centre is via the North Military Road, along
which there is a 'bus service; the return is via the unique triple staircase
exiting onto Snargate Street, almost opposite the marina, but this is subject
to restricted opening times; failing this, the return is via the South Military
Road.

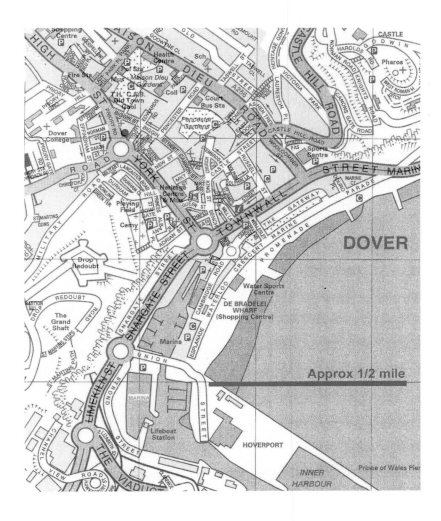

Dover Town Centre

Rail	Dover Priory [3/4M] *[0845 605 0600]*
Buses	Pencester Road: National Express *[0870 580 8080]*
	Stagecoach *[0870 243 3711]*
Taxis	A-B [305006]; heritage [204420]; Star [201010]
Hospital [A&E]	Coombe Valley Rd [A&E 0900-1800hrs] [201624]
Doctor	Dover Health Centre, Maison dieu Rd [865500]
	Peter St Surgery, Peter St [216890]
Dentist	T A Cronin, 6 The paddocks, Maison Dieu Rd [206462]
Police Station	Ladywell [not 24hrs] 240055]
Information Centre	Ladywell [205108]
	www.whitecliffscounttry.org
Museum	Market Square [201066]
Churches CofE	St Mary the Virgin, Biggin St [206842]
RC	St Paul, Maison Dieu Rd [206766]
Methodist/URC	London Rd [206613]
Shops, Pharmacies and Banks	Market square / Biggin St
	24hr convenience store at the Shell Garage, Limekiln St
Supermarkets	Pioneer, High St; Quicksave, Castle St; Tesco, Whitfield [2M]
	Numerous, but including
Public Houses	The Albert, Biggin St [friendly]
	The Eight Bells, Cannon St [predictable Wetherspoons]
Restaurants	There are numerous cafes, bars & restaurants, ethnic & English, including
	Blakes of Dover, Castle St [traditional + B&B] [202194]
	Cullins Yard, Waterloo Crescent [dockside bistro, fish menu] [211666]
	Moonflower, High St [Chinese] [212198]
	'Winston's, Churchill Hotel, Waterloo Crescent [Best Western Group] [203633]
Entertainment	Cinema, Market Square [228000]
	Leisure Centre, Townwall St
Town Events [subject to confirmation	Town Pageant [Spring Bank holiday]
	The Dover Carnival 1st Saturday in July]

Notes: Telephoned enquiries to the Information Centre, other than for accommodation, are merely referred on to a premium rate number. The marina staff are more helpful for casual information .

Town Information   STD Code **01304** *unless otherwise stated*

Approximate Tidal Differences	*As Dover*
Charts	Admiralty SC1698, SC1828; Imray C8, 2100.5; Stanford 1, 9, 19
Weather Forecasts	Marina Office [241663]; Metcall [5 day] *[0906 850 0456]*
Navigation Authority	Dover Harbour Board [24hr] [240400]
	Port Control [24hr] Ch **74**, 12, 16 [206063]
Coastguard	Dover Coastguard Ch **69**, 16 [210008]
Yacht Clubs	Royal Cinque Ports YC, Marine Parade
Marina	terrace, bar, showers, WC
	Dover Marina [24hrs] Ch **80** [241663]
	tidal basin & reception pontoon [min depth 2.4m]
	Granville Dock [usual for visitors] [HW +- 3hrs] [min depth 2.5m]
	Wellington Dock [HW +- 2hrs] [min depth 3.0m]
	lift-out & storage, water, elec, Wcs, showers, laundromat
	pump-out, marine diesel & LPG
	[Transmanche member]
Lift-out & storage	Marina
Fuel	Marina [24hrs] [marine diesel & LPG]
	Shell Garage, Limekiln St [petrol & road diesel in cans]
Calor & Gaz	Sharpe & Enright, Snargate St [206295]
Yards	Dover Yacht Co., Granville Dock[201703 & *07774 966201*]
	repairs and maintenance; M&E engineers
Engineer [M&E]	Mo Parkin, Wellington Dock [210906 & *07836 750060*]
[Electronics]	Grunden Marine, Deal [380962]
Chandlers	Dover Marine Sales, Snargate St [240315]
	inflatable boat repairs, limited general chandlery
	Sharpe & Enright, Snargate St [206295]
	general chandlery, clothing, Calor & Gaz
	Southern Mast & Rigging, Brighton *[01273 818189]*
	Northrop Sails, Ramsgate *[01843 851665]*
Spars & Rigging	Wilkinson Sails, Conyer, N.Kent *[01795 521503]*
Sails	

Notes:

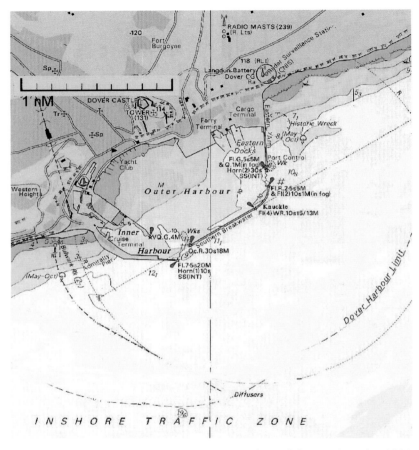

Dover Harbour   Adapted from Admiralty 1828

The small craft holding areas for the west and east entrances are not precisely defined; the ferries have a widely varying angle of approach dependant upon conditions. The approach speed of the Fast Ferries should not be underestimated!

Navigation and Berthing

The Dover Straits are the busiest shipping lane in the world, and Dover Harbour is about the busiest in the United Kingdom. The westbound Traffic Zone is within 4nM of the port entrance, and there is not a lot of scope for manoeuvre by the ferries trying to maintain a timetable; their acceleration from the port, and the speed of approaching 'FastCat' ferries, should not be underestimated. Many yachtsmen view Dover with trepidation, but this is unnecessary given a watchful eye, a well-found boat, and a preparedness to follow the published pilotage information and the clear instructions on VHF from Port Control. Comfort can be taken from the highly professional service, which probably has visiting yachts on radar long before they are likely to cause a problem, and which has fast escort boats at the ready; incidents in the vicinity of the port are very rare indeed.

A night time entry is perfectly feasible. Entry under sail should not be attempted other than in an emergency, and even then only with the cognisance of Port Control who will probably despatch an escort. The useful Dover Marina Visitors' Guide is obtainable by post from the marina [Dover Marina, Dover, Kent CT17 9TF, tel 01304 241663].

The approach from the west is from Dungeness, which is only 3nM from the westbound shipping lane, and also passes the Firing Practice Ranges off Hythe. The passage therefore, will always be *via* the inshore traffic zone on a course of about 048°T, to the small craft holding area at 200m off the western entrance; from close inshore, the only light visible may be that on the nearer arm of the entrance [Fl.7.5s].

Dover Port Control on Ch **74**, 12 or 16 should be advised of entry intentions at about 1nM off; there will be a requirement to report again when at 200m off; if there is single-handed difficulty with the VHF, that too should be made clear. There may well be an instruction to wait for commercial vessels entering or leaving; this may take perhaps fifteen or twenty minutes, in what can be the very uncomfortable conditions of a confused sea, and it is better therefore to furl sails earlier rather than later. There are also the conventional IPT signals [RRR/GWG] on the seaward end of the Admiralty Pier; in the unlikely event of conflicting instructions, clarification must be sought.

The entrance should be made at about midway between the two arms [Fl.7.5s and Oc.R.30s]. On entering, there may be strong cross-tides and a heavy swell but, once inside, the shelter of the wall is a welcome relief; additional care is necessary when tidal heights are below 2m. Initially at least, the centre of the approach channel to the Western Docks should be held, being watchful for any commercial traffic in the vicinity, and the maintenance of a listening watch on Ch **74** is appropriate.

The approach from the east is similarly via the inshore traffic zone, but observing that the Goodwin Sands are within 2nM of South

Foreland. From the South Foreland, standing off a mile or so is a more comfortable avoidance of the beam seas on the final approach, The entry procedure is as from the west; Port Control endeavours to give clearance to yachts ahead of an incoming ferry, but this leaves the possibility of having to abort with a starboard [inshore] turn; it may be necessary also to wait for departing traffic, but waiting outside the eastern entrance inshore usually is not nearly as uncomfortable as at the western. The landmark will be the Port Control tower on the Eastern Arm, and there are IPT signals there also. Entrance should be made midway between the two arms [Fl.R.2.5s and Fl.G.5s].

There is the possibility of using the small boat anchorage in the Outer Harbour; if making for this, Port Control should be advised as soon as they give permission to enter. There is not a lot of water there, but there is good holding in sand other than at a foul area to the immediate east of Castle Jetty. Vessels at anchor should not really be left unattended and, notwithstanding the content of many almanacs, there are no visitors' mooring buoys. It does have the advantages of virtually unrestricted timing for departure, being free of charge, and having the splendid backdrop of Waterloo Crescent and Marine Parade with the beach below. From the centre of the either entrance, there needs to be avoidance of the deep-draught vessel anchorage, the limits of which are well buoyed. Within the Outer Harbour the North Cardinal marking shallow ground [BY] near the western entrance should be left well clear; the relief at making entry should not leave one unaware of traffic.

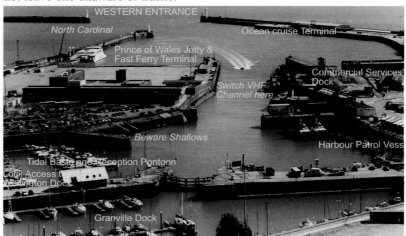

The Western Entrance and the Marinas

Most visitors will wish to use the excellent tidal marina in Granville Dock. From the centre of the western entrance, the course is 291°T for the short leg to leave the old Hoverspeed ramp to starboard, before tucking well into the starboard side of the channel if depth permits. This saves having to be overly concerned at commercial traffic leaving the basins immediately beyond the Admiralty Pier and Cruise terminal; these are mostly tugs and dredgers, but this channel is also used by the Dover Pilots. At this point, there is a large sign requesting contact with DOVER MARINA on **Ch 80** for berthing instructions, but a mobile 'phone call is acceptable [01304 241663]; if a low water departure the next day is planned, it is sensible to request a berth in the tidal basin outside.

The Tidal Basin is on the starboard hand, immediately past the scrubbing berth at the northern end of the old Hoverspeed terminal; at low water, the approach channel is within the white sector of the leading light positioned to the right of the Granville Dock entrance, and care should be taken to avoid the shallows to s'board. Ahead, is a re-

The Tidal Basin

ception pontoon for use by those who have been unable to make contact with the marina; the entrance to Granville Dock is to the left of this, and there is a depth restriction at the sill. In either case, berthing is side-on to pontoon fingers with adequate cleats; the marina office is situated between the Tidal Basin and the Granville Dock, near the swing bridge to the Wellington Dock, and is open 24hrs; a courtesy pack and security code will be issued on reporting in.

On departure, permission is again needed from Dover Port Control. If leaving the marina, liaison with the marina office is appropriate, and permission from Port Control should be requested when the Hoverspeed Terminal is abeam, and stating the entrance being made for; if leaving the anchorage, permission should be sought as soon as way is being made. A departure *via* the eastern entrance may entail a wait adjoining the Knuckle on the Southern Breakwater. It should also be borne in mind that sea conditions outside the harbour will be substantially more severe than inside.

A passage past the port should be made standing reasonably well off to maintain a good view for potential traffic at the entrances. It does no harm to contact Dover Port Control to advise them of intentions, and to request advice as to imminent departures or arrivals. At first sight, there is a lot of detail to assimilate, but this is only a prompt properly to prepare the passage plan; given this, the port presents no great difficulties to the visiting yachtsman, and such a plan will be invaluable at times of restricted visibility.

The Charter of King Charles II   Courtesy Sandwich Guildhall

This is the original of the Charter, hanging on the wall for all to see! A conducted tour of the Guildhall, preferably in a small group, is more akin to being invited into a family home than into a museum.

SANDWICH

SANDWICH, in medieval times, was the premier port of the country, and its history drips from every eaves and oozes from every crack in the pavements; the layout of the small and delightfully confusing central area has changed little, but it still manages to be actively attractive and hospitable; the town is busy in the summer season, but there is no undue emphasis on tourism. The navigation for a visiting yachtsman is unchallenging; the Town Quay still abysmal in spite of some improvements in hand, and the only alternative is some limited upstream berthing.

History

The invading Romans chose Richborough for their island fortress and headquarters, a couple of miles upstream from the present town of Sandwich, and guarding the eastern entrance to the half-mile wide Wantsum channel; after their departure, it was the port of Sarre which took over the service of the Isle of Thanet, with nearby Eastry as the reputed seat of the Kentish kings. Sandwich has no early history, because the sand bank on which it was settled did not rise until the sixth century, and it was slow in developing because of its brackish wells and absence of spring water.

There was a well-established Saxon settlement soon after the sand bank appeared, but the first recorded use of Sandwich as a port and landing place, is that of St. Wilfred in returning from France in 644, and again in 661 on his way to York. It was certainly one of the mustering place for the Norwegians, Danes and Swedes, and was one of the landing places for the Danish attacks of 852; the settlement must have grown rapidly because, although there is little recorded history of those times, it was granted Borough status by King Edgar in the latter half of the tenth century.

A huge Danish force landed in 1006, and threatened the region. Ethelred the Unready bought them off for the staggering sum of £36,000, and proceeded to make preparations for defence; these were paid for by the a levying of a land tax, but the great fleet was affected by storms, and the bulk of it went to London; the town was attacked again in 1009, but this time was bought off for only £3,000. The return in 1011 was only a prelude to the great invasions covering southeast England; in 1016 Sweyn of Denmark was back at Sandwich with his hierarchy, and based himself there for his expeditions throughout Kent. Sweyn's successor, Canute, had respect for the developing churches and, in 1023, made his famous feudal grant of the haven to Christ Church, Canterbury; that survived until the monastic ownership ended in the mid-thirteenth century.

The location provided a shortcut around the notorious North Foreland, and enabled the town's rapid growth. It was the most important trading port in the country at least until the time of the Norman Conquest, and its status was to last for centuries as one of the most important of the Cinque Ports; it attracted the attentions of Harold who, when he came to the throne, seized Sandwich from the monks; St Augustine endeavoured to reclaim it, but it reverted to Christchurch and became the focal point for fights between many factions. When King William I gained the throne, he granted manorial rights over Sandwich to Odo, and the town came to be known as 'Odo's Island' until he was exiled in disgrace; there was some stability emerging because, although there were continuing attacks from Norway and Denmark, the 1054 invasion by Magnus of Norway came to nothing, and the Norse buccaneers who ravished the place in 1084 were beaten off at Thanet.

The Domesday Book records that Sandwich was '*an hundred of itself*', having had at the time of Edward the Confessor a population of 1,800 and 307 houses. At the time of Domesday, the town ranked fourth in the country, after London, Norwich and Ipswich; it had its own mint, and a thriving fishing industry that included attendance at the Yarmouth fair. It was a mustering place for the English fleets on account of its sheltered roadstead, and rendering the same ship service as Dover; it is likely that there was a long-standing alliance with Dover based on the lucrative North Sea herring catches, but William nevertheless reduced the ship service from twenty to five.

The church of St Peter was the town's nucleus, and many of the 383 building plots are traceable today. Strand Street was on the bank of the river, which was then wider; the streets were laid out to provide ten-foot gaps between the buildings, to enable ox carts to pass through the city and outwards *via* the only dry road leading towards Deal; the sea then often swept around the west side of the town as far as the present railway station, and these areas would still be flooded were it not for the Norman sea defences. This was the era of town's major development, and included the construction of the additional parish of St Clement's in around 1100, with its fine Norman tower, tiers of pillars, and rounded arches; it includes a Priest's Room over the north porch, a font of the time of Henry VII, and the Mayor's seat from the time that Mayors were elected there.

The town's history reflected recognition, rather than development, in the twelfth century. In 1155, King Henry II granted its charter. In 1164, St Thomas A'Becket hid at the church at Eastry on his flight to France; the church dates from about 1100, but was rebuilt in the early thirteenth century; in 1170, he returned to a warm welcome by the townsfolk of Sandwich on his way to Canterbury, where he was murdered the next day.

In 1194, King Richard I landed there on his return from imprisonment in Austria and, in thanksgiving, promptly made a barefooted pilgrimage to Canterbury. The disastrous reign of King John and, in particular, the loss of Normandy, impacted on Sandwich as on the other Ports. The French attacked in 1216, and again together with Dover in 1217 on St Bartholomew's Day; on that occasion they were defeated by Hubert de Burgh. St Bartholomew's Hospital in Sandwich had been in existence long before as a hostel for pilgrims, but the Hospital foundation was a thank-offering by the townspeople for their victory, and this remained in favour with the 1349 grant of the tolls of Sandwich ferry.

In the meantime, there was growing friction among King, the ecclesiastical estates, and the town. The town had long been a corporate identity, in that the substantial dues to Christ Church were collected by the town's 'Portreeve' to ensure proper allocation of the liability among the townsfolk and effective self-governance was inevitable with the change in social order. Initially, the power of Christchurch Priory fell to the King and the newly formed town commune who had elected their own Mayor; but this did nothing to assuage the rivalry between the monastic houses. When the Primate died, Pope Innocent III repudiated the nominees from both King and Priory, and commanded Stephen Langton; King John's persistent exclusion of Langton led to the monks being banished, and thereafter their influence waned rapidly. The first recorded Mayoral election was that of Helas [or Elias] de Kingston in 1226 at St Clement's church. In the following year, Sandwich was granted the right to hold a market and to run it together with that of Stonar in accordance with the already established custumal; two years later, Stonar withdrew from the protection of the Abbey, and aligned itself with Sandwich.

Langton died in 1228 and, in 1229, the truce ended between Henry III and the King of France. There was an immediate attempt by France to seize English ships, and the King held to his own use all those at Sandwich capable of carrying at least 16 horses. Sandwich was mentioned in the Cinque Ports list of 1229, when Deal, Walmer, Sarre and Fordwich were also incorporated and, in 1229 Walmer and Ramsgate were appointed as non-Corporate Members. In the following year, control of the Sandwich ships was given to the Bertram de Criel as Constable of Dover Castle, together with Sir Henry de Sandwich as Lord Warden; this was insufficient to prevent Thorold de Kyvilly, the King's Bailiff at Sandwich in 1237, from taking to piracy and he appeared at Shepway on the charge of outlawry, but he survived. In 1248, the port was recognised by Henry III in requiring the 'Mayor and Bailiffs' to equip and provision his fleet; the Mayor's leadership was thus acknowledged in the provision of ship service.

The town continued to expand substantially, and overcame its problem of water supply by channelling the Delf Stream that rose to the south at Worth. The port in this period was far more important than Dover; it was engaged in the wool trade, with conflicts of interests among this, the wine and the general trades. The earliest monastic building of 'Stone House' or the 'Great House' that stood opposite Monken Quay, dated from 1220, and was later occupied by Sir Roger Manhood's School. Warehouses were added between 1225 and 1244 and the 'Herring House' in 1252; the town was one of the major suppliers of fish to the royal households, with the royal purveyor having the first choice of the catch; the quantities consumed were enormous, and supplies could usually be delivered to London within 24 hours. The Priory still retained an important presence, in that it had use of Monken Quay and the Herring House; John Pikenot, cellarer to the Priory, built the Long House in Strand Street between 1253 and 1259 for the monks' occupation. As one monastic establishment waned, so another rose, with the foundation of the White Friars in 1272, although these were little involved in politics.

The Ports strongly supported Simon de Montfort in the Barons' War, largely because of King John's support for Yarmouth, and hence there were frequent changes in the appointments of the Chamberlaincy of Sandwich, the Constableship of Dover Castle, and the Wardenship of the Ports. In 1263, the Ports, notwithstanding their oath to Henry III, treated with Simon de Montfort *about the keeping of the sea* but even his efforts failed to bring about peace between them and Yarmouth; whilst he had a following, Dover remained the only port permitted for cross-channel passages, with Sandwich frozen out of the lucrative trade; when he summoned his first Parliament in 1265, Sandwich was ordered to send four representatives. After the battle of Evesham, the Ports were still trying for greater independence, and in the November of 1265 the King despatched a Yarmouth fleet of 20 ships each with 40 men at arms to police Sandwich; this was not only a political reaction because the Sandwich ship the '*London*' was involved in piracy. The war demonstrated the weakness of divided command between the Constableship and the Wardenship of the Ports, and these offices were combined under Roger de Leybourne in 1265; Prince Edward separated them in the following year, but Roger de Leybourne was left as the superior.

In the late thirteenth century, the Port was struggling to maintain its privileges, notwithstanding the benefits from its Limbs of Stonar, Fordwich, Deal, Sarre and Reculver. The King succeeded in regaining authority over the port and town in 1290 *'for the better defence of the town'*, and appointed his own bailiff, with the Priory retaining its rights upstream and the right to free ferry across the Stour; these arrangements were carefully recorded, with one side being included in the town's custumal, in which it was reserved that it was not answerable '*in the foreign*'. The great storm of 1287, which finally closed the ports of Winchelsea and New Romney, brought further sandbanks to the eastern entrance of the Wantsum, but the silting of the river enabled a widening of the town in the next century, to include new buildings in Strand Street. In 1286, a lay accountant had been appointed and, in the same year, St John's Hospital was founded and was followed by the construction of more quays and the refurbishment of the Long House; a few years later, the town administration was moved to the new building of Castlemead on the south side of Sandown Gate and outside the town's ditch.

The haven continued as a major port for the provisioning of armies, and for trading, with one of the main exports being that of wool. In 1297, 8,563 fleeces and 109 sacks of wool left the haven, and were matched by imports of wines, spices, leather and silks; the King even held his court there to make purchases from the Venetian trading fleet which arrived every four years for that purpose, and there was intense rivalry between Sandwich and London, with Sandwich interrupting and seizing ships so as to claim dues; the river silted progressively from this time, and was not open to remedy. There were numerous cases of piracy; in 1305, the *Snake* of Sandwich patrolled the channel under the orders of the King but, when she boarded a London ship, she lifted part of its cargo that included £250 in specie; the crew of another Sandwich ship, the *St Nicholas*, was accused of having broken all ten Commandments; one John Cole, the Mayor of Sandwich, seized a French vessel at anchor, and put the crew in an unseaworthy hulk bound for Spain, so that they would be in no position to complain; on his retirement, he is attributed as having captured a Flemish ship and taken it to Bruges, where he sold it and its cargo for his own profit. These activities were not surprising at a time when the King was taking twenty percent of the proceeds, and it is even less surprising that complaints to the King brought no retribution; indeed, the prowess was rewarded in 1335 when Peter Barde, the Bailiff of Sandwich, was appointed Admiral of the Cinque Ports.

The Haven recovered some of its cross-channel importance as an embarkation point, when King Edward III in 1342 passed through on his way to Calais with Queen Philippa, and a room in the Old Customs House is known as Queen Philippa's room. The Haven was the main port of embarkation for the battle of Crecy and for the siege of Calais, and '*there never departed out of England before such an army nor so well ordered*'. After Poitiers, the King returned there with his prisoners, the King of France and his son Philip.

There was a great inundation in 1364, in which Stonar was also damaged; the Boarded Groin was built as an embanked sea wall, but Stonar's end was marked by the inundation in 1398. The port still grew in spite of silting at a time when those of Winchelsea and Rye were in terminal decline, and it became hugely important. It was not only continuing to handle a wide variety of goods, including wine, oil, corn, and fruit, but the wool trade justified the appointment of a crown officer in 1364 to oversee the exports; this led to the port briefly being granted the wool staple when it was removed from Queenborough.

In the time of King Richard II, the town had 810 inhabited houses. The defences then relied on the church towers and on the frontages of the houses facing the harbour, but the advent of siege cannons made walling necessary; the town walls were commenced in 1380's, with the Fisher Gate dating from 1384; by the end of the century, all the town gates had been erected, with stone walls to the north side, and a deep and moat and palisade on the landward side. The ancient ramparts almost surrounded the town, although they are now little more than grassy banks; some of the names have early origins, including the Plague Field, the Tannery, the Rope Walk, the Mill Wall, the Bulwark, and The Butts where the archers of Henry V are said to have practised.

In 1385 Charles VI of France assembled his great fleet and army at Sluys for the invasion of England and came to battle in 1387; in the decisive defeat, the ships of Sandwich played their part with five Spanish prizes brought into the Haven. It remained in royal favour, because Richard II borrowed 100 marks from the townsmen in 1397 on the occasion of one of his visits. It was also from around this time that the navigability of the Wantsum was severely restricted, and that both Stonar and Reculver withdrew from membership of the Confederation; in times of difficulty, the town reverted to its usual piracy, resulting in the Lord Warden being ordered to arrest the crew of the *Falcon* in 1406, but little came of it.

The regulations in the 1401 custumal included the provision for 'watch and ward' comprising the patrolling of streets for danger from marauders, and the strict enforcement of a curfew; during the curfew hours, the residents cast their refuse onto the streets for consumption by the pigs and geese, and these were required to be brought in again at the ringing of the 5 a.m. goosebell under the penalty of being impounded. The town still relied on the Delf stream for its water, but by this time it was in a stone lined conduit; the water drawn from the upper reaches was used for drinking, that from a little lower was used for watering animals, and still lower it was used by the industries of tanning and brewing, until it exited from the Town Wall into Gallows Field; there, the stream was used for the drowning of felons.

In 1416, King Henry V stayed at the Whitefriars on his way to Calais; King Henry VI visited too, and recognised its remaining strategic importance by causing further fortification in the form of a gun platform adjoining the Sandown Gate in 1451. This was insufficient to deter the sacking in 1457 by Marshal de Breze and 4,000 men from Honfleur; the attack was from the landward side one Sunday, and was a bloody affair lasting all day until help arrived from the other Ports; the town centre survived, but much of the Norman town was destroyed. There are few remains other than some behind the properties on the south side of Strand Street, but even these probably date from a rebuild after an earlier raid; other than the tower of St Clement's, the outlying areas of St Mary's and St Clement's were destroyed, and much lay ruined for nearly a century; the Mayor was among those killed and, in memory, the Mayors of Sandwich have ever since worn black robes.

The town was again damaged in the dynastic war, and enjoyed the distinction of being one of the worst profiteers among the Ports; this continued into the time of King Edward IV, when a Sandwich crew hired by the people of the east coast for the protection of the herring industry, seized a vessel in Orford Haven and simply towed it away. Under Edward, the town became a prosperous naval and military port, having 95 ships and 1,500 sailors, and he recognised the town's support by granting in the first year of his reign, £100 from customs dues for the fortification and improvement of the port; in 1484 King Richard III renewed a grant of ,100 p.a., but this was surrendered in 1485 and replaced with the grant of 40 sacks of wool per annum to the Mediterranean, provided the town appropriated an equivalent sum plus £20 from its own resources.

The turn of the century saw control over the dredging of oysters, and the joining of Brightlingsea as a non-corporate Member of the Confederation; these events were related to the stagnant trading conditions and economic changes occasioned by the Black Death, and by the further silting of the Wantsum. There are various and disjointed accounts of the ultimate causes of its closure, although it was the same underlying process as that which had created the Goodwin Sands, and was further due to the uncertain sandbanks occasioning the stranding of vessels against which shoals built up. The historian Leland refers to a carrack which sank there in around 1470; the historian Boys refers to a 1483 Spanish wreck to be removed, and to a 1488 order for the Mayor to be granted £40 for the raising of a locally owned 120 ton ship, but these efforts were effectively the end of the fight to save the harbour. In 1513, in making arrangement for the transport of his troops to Calais, Henry VIII was advised that over 60 vessels could lie at Sandwich Quay, and 500-600 in the Haven, but in the event the town provided only one transport attached to the fleet; presumably the Haven fell short of expectations, because Sir Thomas More was commissioned to enquire why it had 'in a few years so sore decayed'. In 1565, the difficulties were blamed conveniently on the innings.

There had been some improvement in trade that enabled the redevelopment of Church Street, and of the outlying parishes together with the repair of St Mary's, all of which had remained derelict since 1247. King Henry VIII visited in 1531, and was petitioned to improve the harbour; the only grants he made were from the proceeds of the sale of local church plate and ornaments. His problems abroad led to the further defences at the Town Quay, and the 1539 construction of the Barbican Gate, but royal patronage gradually shifted to Dover. On the accession of Queen Elizabeth I there were only 65 English merchantmen that the Navy Board regarded as of sufficient size act alongside the Queen's ships. An earlier bounty system was expanded to provide a subsidy of 5s. per ton on all new vessels of over 100 tons; whilst this stimulated national shipbuilding, Sandwich was the only one of the Cinque Ports to respond, and that with the *John* of 140 tons.

In the middle of the sixteenth century it was still an important fishing and trading port, but the effect of harbour silting inhibited much progress and appeals to the crown met with little response. It was still a town with poor water supply and sanitation, open to recurrences of the plague, and affected by the great influenza outbreak; in 1550, the number of inhabited houses had fallen to 200 from the 800 or so in the time of Richard II. The town staged a great welcome for the Queen's visit in 1573, for which it was lavishly decorated; several streets were paved, and 200 townsfolk were caused to be dressed in white doublets to attend on her and her court; whilst the Queen expressed great pleasure at the extravagant hospitality, it resulted in no help.

The town had already benefited from Flemish immigration, and the Queen's sympathy for their cause was the saving of Sandwich. The town petitioned her to allow further immigration, and this she granted to a limit of no more than 300 persons, together with a restriction on their right to trade; this resulted in the new industry of baize and flannel, the introduction of market gardening, and an expansion of commerce to replace that of the haven; the town regained its prosperity, and some Flemish architecture remains. The immigrant families grew to 406 in 1561, and peaked at 2,400 in 1574, but were more than the town could accommodate; even more restrictions were imposed on them, some were moved inland but, within thirty years, only a few remained. They had provided the impetus for economic growth. In 1566, the port could boast of seventeen ships, including one of 40 tons, and sixty-two men; in 1571-72, it had the largest fleet at 36 vessels of any Kentish port, and it remained the second largest in Kent into the 1630's, but this was the end of the medieval port. It continued to decline, but remained as one of local importance for the import of materials for local use, including coal, and bricks and roof tiles from Holland, as well as a continuing trade in food produce

The establishment of Protestantism saw many churches stripped of their ornaments, plate and stained glass; the proceeds were retained in the town, as with the sale of the house of the Whitefriars for £100. The increased level of activity resulted in the restoration of the Fisher Gate in 1560, and the building of the Guildhall in 1579 in which a finely carved Mayoral chair of 1561 is retained. The town's Member of Parliament, Sir

Roger Manhood, founded the Grammar School in 1563 to replace the Chantry School that had closed in 1547; he endowed it with sufficient property for its maintenance, but its ethos was too academic for the day and its reputation was short-lived.

The Manhood School

The Ports, almost all of whom claimed special exemption, resented the levying of ship money by King Charles I in 1637. Sandwich by this time was no longer a port of any consequence, having little left other than a trade with London in coal and corn, but it was a busy agricultural and market town.

In the Civil War of 1642, Sandwich declared for the new order but escaped attack by the Royalist forces; the town gave ready support to the King's execution, and then to the Act of Engagement in 1651, the year in which the Protector, Cromwell, visited. The return of King Charles II was welcomed as his ship lay at anchor awaiting the tide for Dover; the original of his 1668 charter hangs in the Guildhall, as does a part of the 1761 coronation canopy of George III.

The town was not immune from the activities of smugglers, although to a less blatant extent than in southern Kent; even so, the ill-famed Hawkhurst gang had here entered into a written agreement with other gangs to best secure their landing of contraband that was as much as a train of 350 pack horses could carry at a time, and there are numerous cellars and underground passages in the town reputedly used for these operations.

This was symptomatic of the static economy, reflected also in a closed approach to local government. There was little impetus for expansion, but sufficient for the river ferry to become patently inadequate; in 1755, the Corporation obtained Royal Assent for the first bridge over River Stour, and the town was granted the tolls; it was erected at a cost of £1,000, and improved in 1757 with the inclusion of a drawbridge paid for by public subscription; this was a most successful exercise, with the result that the debts had been paid off by the late 1780's. In the early 1780's, the Corporation sold off the city gates for their materials and the proceeds, together with the dues on vessels which maintained a useful coastal trade, were sufficient to embark on a program of paving the streets and providing street lighting; there had been further attempts to raise money for the improvement of the harbour, but these were unsuccessful in the face of competition from Ramsgate; by 1775 all further attempts had been abandoned.

The downstream port of Richborough was used in the Napoleonic times but, whilst Sandwich had always maintained a modest ship building industry, it was never of major importance without the afforested hinterland providing raw materials. There was a modest upsurge with England simultaneously at wars with France and America, and the yard of the Hills family secured the contract for the building of the two brigantines in 1781, the *Falcon* and the *Otter*, each of 202 tons ; the *Weazle* and the *Ferret*, both of the same design, were launched in 1784, and were followed by the *Hound* of 313 tons in 1796. Further orders continued for ever-larger ships until the yard went bankrupt in 1813.

The long overdue Reform Act had little direct effect on enfranchisement within the town, or on the town's Corporation, but it resulted in the municipal boundaries being extended to include Deal and Walmer; it was not until the Municipal Corporations act of 1835 that a more representative elective body was established, but even this failed to address problems of corruption, with election success still passing to the highest spender; inevitably, matters came to a head and Sandwich was for a while disenfranchised. In the economic expansion of the Victorian era, Sandwich fared little differently from many other agricultural market towns although it did, of course, still retain an active harbour and customs house for its coastal trade. The advent of the railway service in 1847 provided further competition for the port, which continued to decline.

The population rose little, remaining at around 3,000, and was a surprisingly young one, with an average age of only 35; the town was slow too, to accept the need for a professional police force or an improved town gaol. The newfound wealth and time for recreation resulted in some over-enthusiastic attention to the restoration of the fabric of the churches, but also the 1895 re-opening of the Grammar School in its splendid new buildings. This was also the time of the foundation of numerous sports clubs including, in 1894, the Royal St George's Golf Club.

In 1916, in the course of the First World War, the port of Richborough was expanded by cutting a canal across a bend in the river to a new wharf just to the north, to form a substantial supply port for the transport of munitions; it was from here that the first roll-on roll-off train ferry was established to carry military supplies to the front. After the War, the town's population expanded steadily, and was self-sufficient in all but manufactured goods; in 1926, the 700th anniversary of the town's Charter was celebrated with a great pageant.

Immediately prior to the Second World War, Richborough was in use as a camp for refugees from Germany. In the course of the War, it was one of those used for the preparation for the Normandy landings, and for the construction of the Mulberry floating harbours. After the War, the Richborough Industrial Estate was revived; the new coal-fired power station was supplied from the wharfage still much in evidence on the riverside, although the power station closed in 1986. Another riverside development is that of the Pfizer pharmaceuticals' company, which arrived in 1954, and expanded dramatically to a workforce of over 3,000.

The Cinque Ports' history is remembered today in the annual ceremony in which the Deputies from Brightlingsea, Fordwich and Sarre attend at the Sandwich Guildhall to pay their ship money. That of Brightlingsea is covenanted at 10s. p.a., and still appears in the town accounts; that of Sarre, at 1s. 8d. has not been paid within living memory, the Deputy's excuse in 2001 being that he had expected to find the money from mooring dues on the Wantsum.

Around and About

A visit to the Information Office in the Guildhall is a priority, as there are several pamphlets available, including those for the Historic Town Trail, for the Guildhall itself, and for the many other attractions. The mere walk up from the river, and a sight of the Elizabethan Guildhall with its well-considered modern extension, should certainly provide a taste for the town.

There are conducted tours of the Guildhall. There are the original Court-Room with its empanelled jury box and Victorian stained glass windows, a good exhibition of Victorian photographs, and further exhibits of the town's past including the original of King Charles II's charter. The tours are conducted mid-week morning and afternoons, and take about an hour, but availability and times vary.

The Guildhall

The Guildhall Courtroom

In the vicinity of the Guildhall are the old gaol house in St Peter's Street, and St Peter's church from which the medieval curfew bell was rung; the church is of thirteenth century fabric with a distinctive 1661 cupola and bone-crypt.

Immediately upstream of the Town Quay is the 1539 Barbican with its flanking bastions at the 1755 bridge over the River Stour, and where tolls were collected until 1977.

A left and right turn leads into Strand Street with its many old dwellings, and particularly that on the corner of Potter Street that was used by the sixteenth century Flemish weavers.

The road continues past Guestling Mill on the right, now converted to residential use, with St Mary's church opposite which is well worth entering; beyond, is a fine street scene of half-timbered houses, with the original 1563 building of the Manhood School almost opposite; off to the right, is the Gallows Field with the Guestling stream used for executions.

The Barbican   The Guestling Mill

A left turn at the site of the old Canterbury Gate leads onto The Butts which were used for archery practice, past the site of the Woodnesborough Gate, below which is the 1392 St Thomas's Hospital for the poor, and then onto the Rope Walk; the setting to one side is very pretty, and there are good townscapes to be seen from the other. At the end of the Ropewalk, is the 1190 St Bartholomew's Hospice and the site of the Newgate, and thence via Mill Wall, over Sandown Road, and onto the Bulwaks dating from 1385. A left turn via Town Wall Path leads past a nicely landscaped area and the old slipway, and left again leads to St Clement's church; here, the town Mayors were elected until 1683, and there are many architecturally decorative features.

A turn down Fisher Street, and across Upper Strand Street, leads to Quay Lane and the old Customs House, with Fisher Gate and its remaining portcullis grooves of fourteenth century origins; beyond is the Town Quay. The walk will take about one hour, allowing no time for distractions.

Quay Lane and Fisher Gate

The White Mill museum, at the far end of Strand Street, is a rare surviving smock mill built in 1760, and now incorporating a museum. It is open on Sundays and Bank Holidays in season.

The Roman fortress of Richborough Castle is a couple of miles upstream, and best visited in season by the regular river bus from near the Stour bridge, although it is just within walking distance from Sandwich. The site is an awesome area of excavations about the central masonry cruciform base of massive construction, all well landscaped and with a good museum. The opening times are seasonal.

The Pfizer Monks' Wall Nature Reserve at Sandwich is a compact area of wetlands attracting numerous indigenous, and frequently rare visiting, birds; the Reserve is reached from the Stour bridge by taking the Ramsgate Road for about a half-mile north, when the access will be found on the left. Access is only by free permit from the town's Information Centre, and is unsuitable for unaccompanied children.

The Town Quay

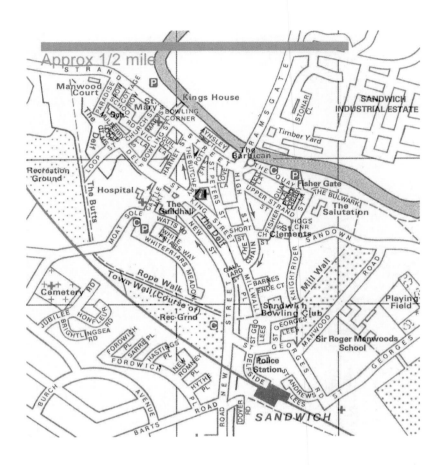

Sandwich Town Centre

Rail	Sandwich, New Street [1 mile] *[0845 748 4950]*
Buses	National Express *[0870 580 8080]*; Stagecoach *[0870 608 2608]*
Taxis	Airport Direct [615408]; Sandwich Cars [617424]; Stour Cars [612897]

Hospital [A&E]	Q.E.Q.M., Broadstairs Road, Margate *[01843 225 544]*
Doctor	Market Place Surgery [behind Guildhall] [613436]
Dentist	N. Dymant, Moat Sole [617131]
Police [office hours only]	Cattle Market [612214]

Information Centre [seasonal]		Guildhall [613565]
Museum		Guildhall [617179]
Churches	C of E	St Clement's, Church Street [613138]
	R C	St Andrew's, St George's Road [37480]
	Methodist / URC	Woodnesborough Road [372002]

Shops and Banks	High Street, Cattle Market, and otherwise scattered
Pharmacy	Pioneer Supermarket, Moat Sole
Supermarket	Pioneer, Moat Sole [behind Guildhall]
	Spar, High Street

Public Houses	The George and Dragon [good food] Fisher Street
	King's Arms [seafood platter] Strand Street
	The Bell Hotel [large and very busy in season] Town Quay
	New Inn [decent food] Delf Street
Restaurants	Most public houses serve food, and there are some cafes
	Restaurants include
	Fishermen's Wharf [brasserie] Barbican [613636]
	Number Six [bistro style] High Street [614949]

| Entertainment | Cinema, Delf Street |

| Town Events [subject to confirmation] | Royal St Georges [July] |

Notes: Avoid the Royal St Georges week, unless it is of particular interest

Approximate Tidal Differences:

Sandwich, Dover +01hr 00; Pegwell Bay, Dover +00hr 20

Charts   Admiralty, 1828

Weather Forecast   Metcall [5 day inshore] [09068 500 456]

Navigation Authority   Sandwich Port and Haven Commissioners, Guildhall [617197]

Stour Bridge access [207707 - daytime] [07860 378792 - 24hrs]

Coastguard   Dover [01304 210008]

Berthing   Town Quay [no direct contact possible]

slipway, water, public WC [not 24hrs]

Yard   Highway Marine, Strand Street [613925]

crane [3T, or over by arrangement],

limited pontoon berths, storage, mech. engineer, minor repairs, water

Fuel   Petrol and road diesel in cans from garage [nr. rlwy. stn., 1M]

Calor   Highway Marine, Strand Street [Not Gaz] [613925]

Chandlers   Highway Marine, Strand Street [613925]

General Repairs   Highway Marine, Strand Street [Minor repairs] [613925]

Engineers   Mechanical   Highway Marine, Strand Street [613925]

Electrical & VHF Grunden Marine [Deal] [380962] [07815 120340]

Spars and Rigging   Southern Mast and Rigging, Brighton [01273 818189]

Davis Marine, Military Road, Ramsgate [01843 586172] [07977 494855]

Sails   Wilkinson Sails, Conyer [N.Kent][01795 521503]

Northrop Sails, Military Road, Ramsgate [01843 851665]

Notes: Highway Marine are enthusiastically helpful, but cater mostly for craft of up to say 7 or 8m.

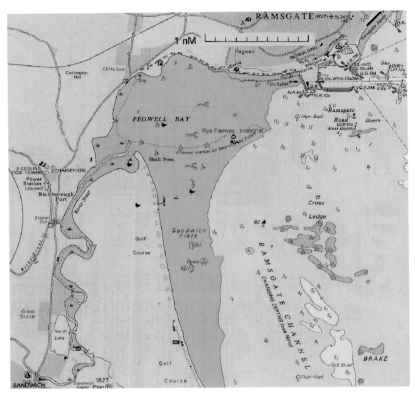

Pegwell Bay and the River Stour   Adapted from Admiralty 1828

This is the historic Pegwell Bay. It is helpful first to identify *Fairway* but, on the top of springs for most craft, navigation by depth sounder is adequate; it is simply a matter of heading for the shore, turning north, and following the contour around the Ness.

Navigation and Berthing

The entrance to the River Stour is from Pegwell Bay, where there is little water, and possibly insufficient on some neaps. Once *Stour Fairway* has been identified, the channel is well marked and, upstream of the Ness, there is better water. Without familiarity, entry is not really feasible under sail, and should not be attempted in conditions of poor visibility.

The approach from the south is from *Deal Bank* [Fl.(2)R.5s], and *via* the inshore Ramsgate channel on a course of 347°T for 5.2nM to the *No2* buoy [G, unlit]; from here the course is 340°T for 0.9nM across the bay to the small *Stour Fairway* [RW, unlit, seasonal] [51° 18.89N 001° 23.51W, but subject to relocation]; the short leg across the Flats dries to about 1.5m above chart datum.

The approach from the north is from the Ramsgate Port holding area at the South Breakwater, on a course of 250°T for 1.2nM or, more precisely, from the west cardinal *West Quern* [YBY, Q.(9)], to *Stour Fairway*, and parts of this leg dry to about 2m above chart datum. In each case, location of *Stour Fairway* is assisted by holding the power station tall chimney in transit with the leftmost of the three cooling towers; this transit is imprecise, because of the size of the structures. The depths noted are also imprecise, because of the combination of shifting sands and continuing silting; at *Stour Fairway* there is currently 3.0m at HWN.

The Entrance to the River Stour
*Note the port-hand structure on the extreme left,
the st'bd hand buoy and the transit on the power station*

The course from *Stour Fairway* is a little south of west, and turning gently west; the first 0.5nM is buoyed to a starboard hand scaffold tower beacon with unlit topmark; thereafter, the course is well marked by withies on both hands through the horseshoe around Shellness; upstream, the course is clearly defined, passing the wharfage to the disused power station, the Stonar Cut to the disused Port of Richborough, a small berthing facility adjoining an industrial estate, and the extensive Pfizer plant, all on the starboard hand. The industrial views provide a commentary on modern history but, for a pastoral scene, eyes should be kept on the left bank.

The distance from the Ness to Sandwich is about 4nM, and follows a gently winding course; speed should be kept to a minimum to avoid damage to the banks. At Sandwich, there is the choice between berthing at the Town Quay, and proceeding upstream to staging and finger jetties on the starboard hand immediately above the bridge.

At the Town Quay, a mud bank adjoins the wall and the best water is to be found towards the bridge; the 30m or so immediately below the bridge are occupied by the slipway and a water-tours boat; there is ample space to turn. The Quay wall is rough, with projecting galvanised ladders, non-slip concrete bollards, and iron rings set into the adjacent public car park, but improvements are in hand; there is no supervision, and rafting up may well be necessary, albeit resented by the residents. Fender boards and plenty of fenders are the first requirement, followed by shore lines and springs to accommodate the tidal range of about 2.5m, and an eye open for the ladders; it is advisable to use the rings provided to tie the mast back for the first tide. It is unlikely that a charge will be made, with the only facilities being the cold-water tap at the nearby public convenience [not 24hrs].

Sandwich Town Quay -
Upstream View

Sandwich Town Quay -
Downstream View

On departure, it should be remembered that there is always water in the Stour at this level, and timing therefore must be with Pegwell Bay in mind.

Ramsgate - the Inner Harbour

At one time, the Inner Harbour was packed with over a hundred fishing vessels. The site of the old Ice House is no longer in evidence.

RAMSGATE

RAMSGATE is for relaxation, where the entertainment opportunities are undemanding. The harbour and marina provide easy access, decent facilities and a friendly welcome, all against a fine backdrop.

History

The 'gates' or gaps in the chalk cliffs have connotations of the Frisian '*seegats*' that attracted the early settlements, and the Roman remains suggest that Ramsgate was a small port ancillary to Richborough. It is Pegwell Bay which is notable; Hengist and Horsa landed there at the behest of King Ethelbert in 449, with the site now marked by a replica longboat sailed from Norway to commemorate the 1,500th anniversary; nearby at Ebbsfleet is the 597 landing place of St. Augustine, commemorated by a roadside cross erected at Cliffsend; it was also the base for the first commercial Hovercraft service.

The settlement of Ramsgate merited no mention in Domesday. At that time the churches of St Peter, St John and St Laurence were all simply referred to as 'in Thanet', and were the nuclei of what were to become Margate, Broadstairs and Ramsgate. St Laurence was the southernmost and the nearest to the Ramsgate of today and, with the town's development, it became a parish in its own right in 1275. The development of Ramsgate was in the natural hollow where York Street now stands, rising to South Cliff on one side and to Albion Cliff on the other, with King and Queen Streets now over the old natural channels. It was always a fishing port with a breakwater dating from the fourteenth century, and important to the supply of Thanet; there is little further history until well into the fifteenth century.

In 1444, it contributed to the claims made on Sandwich on the occasion of Henry VI's marriage and, by 1483, it was already associated with Sandwich for the purposes of the Confederation. The town limits were then described as '*The bounds of the Liberty of the Cinque Ports at Ramsgate: Imprimis, a vie vocata steyeres way In the south, et sic directe usque Buntygez: et abinde per viam communum usque quandam crueem vocatum Thackers Cross: et abinde usque moliendum ventribicum: et abinde per viam communum usque Middleton's Crosse: et abinde directe per le veridem lynche usque fossatum maris*'. In 1495, it was noted that contributions towards ship service were Sandwich, 6s.8d., with Ramsgate, Fordwich, Sarre, and Deal and Walmer each contributing 3s.4d.; the total of 20s. was rather less than 1/3 of that of all the Ports. In 1556 Ramsgate contributed £8 towards the sum which Sandwich was called to pay towards the raising of armed forces by the Lord Warden '*to go to the wars*'. At that time, the town comprised 25 houses, 40 boats and fishing vessels, and 70 men employed in fishing and in the transport of grain. It possessed only a small breakwater to give protection to a small fleet of fishing vessels of two to sixteen tons; this was insufficient to encourage economic growth, let alone contribute to the Confederation, and it must therefore have relied largely on its agricultural activities, as with the other Margate villages.

A 1560 ecclesiastical survey defined the boundaries of Ramsgate as '*The sea lyeth on the East side of our Liberties, and on the South side from the sea towards the West a way called Thomas Tarryes Way, leading to a close called Nynnes Close, and so leadeth by a close called Beysants, and so down through Ellington: and so the way leadeth towards the South part of Ramsgate Mill and so to a way that leadeth between Herston and Ramsgate: and so on that way up to the end of Jellyngham Hill and so on to the sea cliff - a way six foot broad*'. A survey in 1565 found 98 households, meaning farmhouses as distinguished from cottages, but another writer gave it as 25 houses and 98 persons as including St Laurence, '*it being only a small fishing place*'. It was of sufficient importance to justify the levying of dues and droits on all using the pier and harbour from 1578; this was enforced through its association with the Confederation, and only by continuing appeals to the Lord Warden. By the seventeenth century, although the town was still governed by a Magistrate appointed by Sandwich, as a non-corporate member it made no further contributions.

In the mid seventeenth century, the port benefited only indirectly from the growing Baltic trade, although having provided several mariners for the exploration of that region, and as having become known also as a home for retired mariners. The growing international trade encouraged some expansion, when the harbour benefited from attending on the ships waiting in the Downs, and notably those of the East India Company; the service was known as 'foying' and 'hovelling', and the town had the advantage of its agricultural community for the provision of fresh produce. The vessels used were known as 'hoys', which were spacious cutters, the larger ones being between 70 and 100 tons; they not only acted as lighters to carry the trade into London, a passage which would take some 24 to 36 hours, but were also served Thanet where the roads were still very poor.

This was the time of town's first period of sustained expansion, and properties in the vicinity of York Street are traceable back to the sixteenth and seventeenth centuries; later, there was the removal of the solid cliff for the development of Kent Terrace, but then there was not even a beach. The town's first Poor House was built in King Street in 1726, but this has disappeared.

In 1715 the most recent additions to the East Pier, although in stone, were sufficiently storm damaged to encourage the timber construction of the new West Pier; a great storm in 1748 led to the Government deciding on Ramsgate as a harbour of refuge. The cliffs were by then an inconvenience to access between the growing residential areas on the cliff top, and in 1754, a carpenter by the name of Jacob Steed constructed a timber stairway linking the harbour with the upper levels; it was subsequently resited in stone to the present design, but is still known as Jacob's Ladder. This was much used by smugglers, particularly for smaller items such as coin and plate, for transfer to Deal and thence by rowing boat across the channel, and this trade continued into the nineteenth century.

The prevailing south westerlies presented difficulties to the sailing vessels entering the harbour, as they needed to carry as much sail as necessary to maintain steerage, but their momentum was uncontrollable. In the 1750's, a signal flagstaff was erected on the front near the present Foy Boat Inn to indicate the depth of water; a red flag indicated, not an insufficiency of water, but an insufficiency of exposed mud bank onto which the ships could ground gently; the Foy Boat Inn was one of the earliest establishments, but was rebuilt after the second World War.

A survey in 1752 found that the laboriously improved harbour was silting up, and John Smeaton of Eddystone Lighthouse fame was called in; over 52,000 tons of silt were removed, but it was still a losing battle. In contrast to many of the other Ports, professional recommendations were largely adopted, and this led to the continuous cross-wall arrangement that is the outline of the present inner harbour; this tidal basin incorporated sluice holes at its base that, at low water, effectively scoured the outer harbour, but these works were not completed before 1779. This was the period which saw the emergence of professional fishermen, and hence the works were augmented in 1788 with a 340ft extension to the East Pier, and, by 1791, the harbour could accommodate over 130 vessels; Smeaton's design for a dry dock had also been implemented, together with an additional lighthouse in 1795 and, from 1802, the stationing of a lifeboat.

It was Ramsgate's combination of port and agriculture that enabled sustained growth, and was catalysed by the novelty of f sea bathing. The town never competed seriously with Margate simply because most visitors arrived from there by sea from London, and it was a further twenty years before an Act was passed for the town's paving, lighting and cleansing. At the same time, the Market House was built, and was used for the Council meetings that had hitherto been held variously in the Poor House and in public houses, and the first license was granted for a Playhouse.

This was Ramsgate's second period of sustained growth, to be reinforced by the Napoleonic threat, and which was to take it into the nineteenth century. The 550ft timber West Pier was found to have been damaged by Teredo worm, and was replaced with stonework; its original lighthouse, having been built too close to the entrance and often damaged by the yardarms of vessels, was also rebuilt. The Military Road was improved for the deployment of the thousands of troops encamped around the tow, the beaches were used extensively for cavalry training, and the cliffs for target practice; this enormous influx of personnel impacted dramatically on trade. In the years 1788-89 the Ramsgate chapel, built privately as a chapel of ease, became permanent and was the foundation of St Mary's church; 1789 saw the development of Albion Place and Albion Hill to the west of the harbour, and expansion progressed into the 1820's when the West Cliff area was developed too. The Grammar School that been founded in 1797 in Townley Street by Dr. William Humble, was rebuilt in 1817 after several moves, and again in 1879 with its splendidly Victorian facade.

Ramsgate was sufficiently fashionable to warrant the visit there by King George IV in 1821, *en route* for Calais; on his return, a year later, a grateful town commemorated the visit by the erection of an obelisk in Dublin Granite, which stands at foot of the East Pier. It was not until 1827 that Ramsgate achieved ecclesiastical separation from Parish of St Laurence, and was followed by the erection of St George's Church on Church Hill.

In 1815, the Astronomer Royal laid a meridian line laid at the foot of the East Pier. Two years later, the Clockhouse was constructed on the same line, and it is in use today as the Maritime Museum; outside, is the diving bell used in the repair of east pier; the inscription above the entrance denotes Ramsgate Mean Time as 5 minutes and 41 seconds ahead of Greenwich Mean Time, and was used until 1848 when G.M.T. was adopted for the 'convenience of shipping'; many towns then had their own 'mean time', a system which was only abandoned with the advent of railway timetabling. In 1838, Morton constructed his Patent Slipway at East Pier, and it is still in use.

Ramsgate was a small shipbuilding centre, and one of the oldest yards was that of Miller Hinds and Beeching, established from around 1800. The new steam hoys were coming into commission, and could make London in less than twelve hours against the 24 to 36 hours by sail; just as the demand for the sailing hoys was falling, the Devon trawlers made their appearance, attracted by the absence of fishing dues, a good harbour, and a good market; these fishermen confined their activities to the winter months, and merely landed their catches rather than settling. Most of the town's fishing had been inshore, using drift nets from two or three masted luggers with a medieval sail rig, and with a crew of two or three; these craft were best suited to inshore waters, but the Brixham vessels were deep-sea smacks, and some came to be purchased by Ramsgate fishermen. The construction of the new locally built smacks reflected their Devon counterparts, but were around 50 ft and 40 tons, somewhat beamier and with a lower transom to assist in net hauling; they were all built in oak from the forests around Canterbury and, as the larger scantlings became unavailable, there was introduced the scarfed two-piece keel in elm. With the local fishermen venturing further into the North Sea, the vessels incorporated an open well that accounted for around one-third of the hull volume and overcame the problem of keeping the catch fresh.

The middle of the century saw some sixty smacks using Ramsgate as a base for the North Sea. The trade was hampered by the shortage of ice for onwards transportation, as most was weather dependent and collected from ponds by local farmers; some of the more adventurous fishermen excluded the middlemen, by sailing their catch up the Thames for sale directly off the boats, and these auctions were usually held at public houses, as at the 'Town of Ramsgate' in Wapping High Street. The process of ice manufacture was still unknown, but the situation changed with the importation of ice from Scandinavia; ice houses were constructed at the harbour, having 8ft thick walls, and typically storing 8,000 tons; even Smeaton's dry dock was so converted. The ships' wells were also converted for packing the catch at sea.

This expansion of the industry led to the Board of Trade levying dues on all vessels, with the inevitable result of some returning to Brixham and some locals relocating to the Yorkshire coast; in 1863 therefore, the number of locally registered trawlers fell to fifty. This reduction was short-lived, resulting in 139 being locally registered in 1873, and rising to 185 between 1870 and 1890; these numbers were augmented by visiting fleets from Devon, Deal, Rye, and Lowestoft, to a total of over 300 vessels, and the largest collection in the country with peak catches of over 70,000 fish; this was all very different from the findings of an 1833 enquiry into the condition of the channel fisheries in which Ramsgate was not even mentioned. The Ramsgate fishing industry towards the end of the century was renowned for both the volume and the quality of its catches; thus, of the fleets between Dungeness and Margate in 1895 whose total catch was over 810 tons, Ramsgate's share was near 45% at an average price of £2.2s. per cwt., compared with the average price at Dungeness of only 10s. per cwt., and Ramsgate therefore was ahead of Lowestoft.

The railway arrived in 1846, and a direct connection with London was made in 1859; this further encouraged the town's growth, both in terms of the local industries and of the holidaymakers. The social implications of the disparity in wealth among the townspeople were not overlooked, in that the welfare provisions for the sailors and 'smack boys' were addressed by Canon Eustace Brenan, the vicar of Christ Church, and who founded the 'Sailors' Church and Harbour Mission' in 1878; the resulting mission was built at the foot of Jacob's Ladder, as a chapel on the ground and accommodation for the smack boys above; the mission evolved into receiving rescued sailors, but it is no longer in use as such, merely providing pleasant quietude and a few sailing exhibits.

The town's population reached 22,683 in 1881 and, surprisingly, it was not until then that the local Fishmarket was built; also in that year, the Ramsgate Promenade Pier Company built a timber leisure pier with music hall entertainment but, in 1918, this fell to two fires, a drifting trawler, and a mine; in the meantime, there had been the 1903 opening of the Royal Victorian Pavilion. It was only in 1884 that the town was incorporated; previously, it was still under the jurisdiction of the Recorder at Sandwich, and received its Deputy from there.

The First World War had little direct impact on the town except for the stationing there of the Dover Patrol, but many fishermen moved away after the Fishmarket was bombed by a Zeppelin; after the War, there were attempts to establish a steam trawler fleet, but these failed in the face of competition from Grimsby. During the Second World War, the harbour was again used by the Dover Patrol, and two further small slipways were constructed at East Pier for naval and RAF craft; No 27 Air Sea Rescue unit was billeted at the Royal Oak Hotel, and is credited with having saved over 13,000 lives; in the harbour is the motor launch '*New Britannic*', which took part in the Dunkirk evacuation, rescuing 3,000 troops from the beach and ferrying them to waiting warships and, in all, some 82,000 troops returned to England *via* Ramsgate. The nearby airfield at Manston was built for the war, and is now a commercial airfield with a museum of wartime exhibits.

The post-war era was marked by a progressive decline in the fishing industry, and there are few such vessels remaining in the harbour. The several ferry services operating in response to increased demand for cross-channel traffic, including the Hovercraft from Pegwell Bay, all fell eventually to competition from Dover but, from 1976, there has been a steady development in leisure moorings leading to the construction of the west marina in 2000. The outer commercial harbour was constructed in 1987, but has remained of limited use; the passenger ferry service has been discontinued, but there remains the commercial RoRo service.

Around and About

Around the town, there are few buildings predating the nineteenth century, and little of historic interest without embarking on detailed re-search. The Fishermen's Church merits a visit, and an ascent via Jacob's Ladder leads to the pleasant West Cliff Royal Esplanade with its views, and

with the Model Village and Motor Museum nearby. Below is the decep-
tively busy commercial ferry service whilst, off to the west, is the Priory.

The Clockhouse Maritime
Museum provides interest for a
couple of hours; there is the
'Harbour Trail' leaflet available,
providing a guide to historic buildings and other places of interest in
the vicinity. Within the Dock are
several preserved vessels, some of
which are open to visitors; these
include a couple of the Dunkirk
'Little Ships', including the *New*

The Clockhouse Museum

Britannic that alone rescued 3,000 troops, a classic smack or two, and the
Cervia, about the last of the steam tugs to be built.

Ramsgate provides many entertainment facilities, from the
beaches through the Casino, theatre and cinema, to family attractions. It is
much under-rated for a quiet stay.

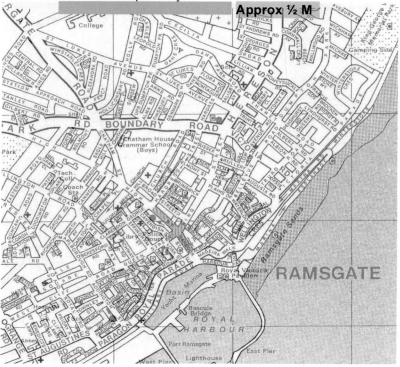

Ramsgate Centre

Rail	Ramsgate, [above High St] [2M from centre] *0845 748 4950*
Buses	National Express *[0870 608 2608]*
Taxis	Dee-Lux [589589]; Invicta Cars [585585]; Star [581581]
Hospital [A&E]	Queen Elizabeth the Queen Mother, Margate [225544]
Doctors	69 Addington Street [593544]
	The Grange Medical centre, West Cliff Road [595051]
Dentists	S M Ali, 131 high St [592421]; J Hamill, 73 Hereson Rd [581666]
Police Station	26 York St [restricted hours] [231055]
Information Centre	Albert Court, York St [583333]
	www.tourism.thanet.gov.uk
Museum, Maritime	The Clock House, Royal Harbour [570622]
Churches C of E	St George's, Church Hill [off High St] [593593]
RC	St Augustine's Abbey Church, St Augustine's Rd [593045]
Methodist / URC	Hadras Street United [off King Street] [852057]
Shops	Numerous in High St, King St and Queen St
Pharmacy	High St
Banks	High St & Queen St
Supermarkets	Budgens, High St; Waitrose, Queen St
Yacht Club	The Royal Temple Y C, Sion Hill [571766]
	www.rtyc.co.uk
	bar, terrace, dining [seasonal], accommodation
Public Houses	Numerous of similar ambience, and most serve food; try
	The Royal Temple Y C [splendid terrace]
	The Horse & Groom, Charlotte Ct [York St] [unpretentious]
	Jackson's Wharf, York St [cafe style]
Restaurants	There are numerous cafes & restaurants, but few for gourmets; try
	The Churchill Tavern, The Paragon [conventional] [587862]
	The Royal Temple Y C [571766]
	Numerous on Sion Hill
	The Harbour Lights, East Pier [basic, good value, fine view]
Entertainment	Granville Theatre & Cinema, Victoria Parade
	Grosvenor Casino, East Pier
	Swimming Pool, Newington Rd [493754]
	Sports & Leisure Centre, High St [585111]
	Model Village & Motor Museum, West Cliff
Town Events [subject to confirmation]	Street Markets [Fri & Sat]

Notes:

Town Information   STD Code **01843** *unless otherwise stated*

Approximate Tidal Difference	Dover +00hrs 20
Charts	Admiralty 1827 & 1828; Imray 2100.5, C1, C8; Stanford 5 & 9
Weather Forecast	Marina Office; Metcall [5 day] *[0968 500 456]*
Port Control	Harbour Office, Military Rd [572100]
	Ramsgate Port Control [24hr] [Ch14] [572112]
Coastguard	Dover *[01304 210008]*
Marina	Royal Harbour [24hrs] [Ch80] [572100]
	www.ramsgatemarina.co.uk
	lift-out & storage, towage, water, elec, WC/showers, launderette
	fuel barge, scrubbing grid
	Inner Harbour HW +/- 2hrs; facilities as for Royal Harbour
Fuel	Marina pontoon
Calor & Gaz	Bosun's Locker, Military Rd [597158]
Yard	Dover Yacht Co, Granville Dock, Dover *[01304 201073]*
	[07774 966201]
	general repairs, mech & elec engineers

Chandlers		Bosun's Locker, Military Rd [597158]
General repairs		Davis Marine Services, Military Rd [586172]
Hull repairs	Wood	R Cannon & Sons, Military Rd *[078702 05647]*
	GRP	Davis Marine Services, Military Rd [586172]
	Steel	A & P, East Pier [slip] [593140]
Engineers	Mechanical	Marlec Marine, Military Rd [852452]
	M & E	Davis Marine , Military Rd [586172]
	Electrical & VHF	Grunden Marine, Deal *[01843 855166]*
		Mobile & Marine Radio Tech,
	VHF	High St, St Laurence [594594]
Sails		Northrop Sails, Military Rd., Ramsgate [8516655]
		Wilkinson Sails, Conyer [N Kent] *[01795 521503]*
Spars & Rigging		Davis Marine, Military Rd [586172]
		Southern Mast & Rigging, Brighton *[01273 818189]*

Notes:

Ramsgate Harbour and Approaches   Adapted from Admiralty 1828

Unlike Dover, the small craft holding areas are specific. Note the pre-ferred crossing of the main channel just west of *No 3*

Navigation and Berthing

A comprehensive guide is available from the Harbour Office. The navigation is undemanding; entry into the, fairly well sheltered, outer harbour is can be made under sail but progress thereafter should be under engine. There are frequent RoRo movements operating from the outer commercial harbour, and; Pilot vessels, the Lifeboat and minor commercial traffic and inshore fishing boats operate from the Royal [main, inner] Harbour. There is plenty of sea room, but the Port Control signals and procedure are to be obeyed. The notes below are mostly as already described for Sandwich.

The inshore passage from Deal is best made with *Deal Bank* left to port. The course is then 347°T for 5.2nM for the green *B2* that marks the western edge of the Cross Ledge shoals and which should therefore be left to starboard. The course is then 036°T for 1.6nM for the eastern point of the harbour's South Breakwater and small craft holding area; on this leg, the minimum charted depth is 2m, but an eye should be kept on the depth sounder and the west cardinal *West Quern* [Q(9)15s] should be left well clear. Care must be taken to identify the cardinals in the vicinity.

The offshore passage is near direct by leaving *Deal Bank* close to port, on a course of 022°T for 4.4nM to *Brake* [Fl.(4)R.15s] immediately on the port hand, with the west cardinal *North West Goodwin* [Q(9)15s] to starboard. The course from *Brake* can safely be anything between 330°T for 2.8nM and 000°T for 2.4nM, to intersect the southern limit of the well buoyed main entrance channel, at which a parallel course of 270°T leads into the small craft holding area; the more precise course from *Brake* is 333°T for 2.4nM to the north cardinal *North Quern*, from which the course is again 270°T for the small craft holding area.

The approach from the north is best made commencing about 0.7nM off the North Foreland cliff face, and when the North Foreland Lighthouse [Fl.(5)WR.20s] bears 270°T. The course from here can be between 180°T for 2.9nM and 202°T for 3.0nM to intersect the northern limit of the well buoyed entrance channel, at which a parallel course of 270°T leads into the small craft holding area; in the immediate vicinity is *No 3* [Fl.G.2.5s], and the opportunity should be taken to identify the north cardinal *North Quern* to the southwest, and the south cardinal *No 5* to the immediate west. The north holding area is about 0.6nM offshore to avoid the shoals, and is exposed to the southwest.

Navigation is assisted by the east-west orientation of the entrance channel; the charted depths are not maintained, although this is of only academic interest to the yachtsman. The final approach from either holding area requires observance of the IPT signals above the building at the inshore end of the northern breakwater [RRR or GGG, & Fl.Or for manoeuvring ferries], and above this are the port control office and signals;

the clutter of town lights can make the signals difficult to identify. Contact should also be made with Ramsgate Port Control on VHF Ch14 [or telephone on 01843 572112], which is at the least helpful for their radar identification. After a departing RoRo, the signals may remain RRR until the vessel is long clear, but permission may be given for a yacht to enter in the meantime; some fishing vessels ignore the signals, but it is better not to follow their example.

From the north holding area, the recommended small boat track crosses the main entrance channel at right angles [180°T] to the south side of this channel, and then on 270°T towards the entrance, keeping just south of *North Quern*; from the south holding area, the recommended track follows a turn to port, to coincide with that from the north holding area; a watch needs to be kept for small craft exiting around the end of the breakwater.

Rounding *Harbour*

The *Ro-Ro* Terminal to the West

The entrance should be made midway between the two breakwaters [VQR & QG], on a course of 310⁰T to about parallel the north breakwater, and continued until the entrance to the Royal Harbour is well open. At this point a turn onto 020⁰T will leave *Harbour* [QG] to starboard to make the entrance; this is important. At anything below half-tide, the port hand should be well favoured to avoid the drying bank beneath the East Pier.

Ramsgate Harbour Entrance, with the Marina to the West

It is helpful to contact Ramsgate Marina on VHF Ch 80 [or telephone on 01843 572100] for berthing instructions, from any position past *Harbour*. The modern West Marina will be found to port, with finger pontoons and an adequacy of cleats; in the absence of directions, it is acceptable to take the most convenient berth available unless it is marked 'reserved'. There are limited but useful WC facilities on the pontoon, but the usual welcome pack and security codes are issued on reporting in to the marina office.

In the unlikely event of the West Marina being full, directions will be given to the old East Marina with similar facilities, although this is usually retained for residents; the course will be along the outer side of the West Marina, before a starboard turn into the berthing. The locked Inner Harbour is also occupied predominantly by residents, and is slightly cheaper for a long stay; for locking times [approx HW +/-2hrs] the Marina office should be contacted, and the signals above the lock gates obeyed; if necessary, any available outer berth may be used whilst waiting. Manoeuvring within the harbour requires awareness of the drying East Bank lying between the East Marina and the East Pier, buoyed only at its western edge [Fl.G], but there is a maintained channel around its perimeter.

The marina does become full during Ramsgate week; it is better then to arrive early, before the races have finished!

Faversham - Oyster Bay House

The Oyster Bay Company was one of the earliest to be incorporated. Its robustly Victorian warehouse is a landmark facing Faversham Creek, and has now been skillfully converted to home and offices.

FAVERSHAM

FAVERSHAM, as a small, accessible and friendly town with a wealth of interest, must be Kent's best-kept secret; it is still a town run for itself rather than for tourists and, just as the Romans bypassed it with Watling Street, so it has also escaped the excesses of modern development. The shortcomings of restricted tidal berthing should not deter any mariner worth his salt.

History

The natural agricultural resources in proximity to both fresh water and the Thames estuary, led to Faversham having been settled from the earliest of times. The Romans were the first of whom there are records, although they bypassed it with Watling Street; the Jutes subsequently settled it and, even in those days, it was a place of importance as evidenced by the extent and quality of burial artefacts, many of which are in the British Museum. There is little known of the town's early history but, in Saxon times, only it and Newenden were holding regular markets in Kent, and that of Faversham was to gain regional importance. It was also from the town's edge that King Whitred of Kent declared the churches and monasteries exempt from public taxation, and it was in the contemporary charter that there were first mentioned the boundaries of the town, the port, and the oyster fisheries; those of the oyster fisheries were then handed down orally, until they were first written in 1599.

The time of Edward the Confessor saw the town as already having acquired some status, because it shared responsibility for the defence of the 'Narrow Seas', and enjoyed royal favour. In 1070, William the Conqueror granted an advowson for a new church in the town; the result was the foundation of the present-day Church of St Mary, then of a long, narrow and conventional Norman style. Unlike its important near neighbours of Whitstable and Reculver, the access to the town's port *via* the River Swale provided protection from cross channel raiding and, notwithstanding the Danes' earlier interest in the Isle of Sheppey, William regarded fortification as unnecessary.

There was progressive coastal subsidence in this era leading to extensive flooding, and the original port was therefore constructed at Thorne, on high ground a little downstream from the town, but it was later washed away by the tides. King Stephen landed there, both Dover and

Canterbury having held out against him; in recognition, he patronised the building of Faversham Abbey in 1147, thus prompting an economic expansion from which the town grew around the four roads radiating from St Anne's Cross, and the town quays were revitalised. The Abbey was granted the lordship of the manor, which included the fishing rights bounded by Kimber Creek and Reculver, together with those over many of the extensive and hitherto uncontrolled oyster beds.

There is no mention of Faversham in the Saxon Chronicles until the death of Stephen in 1154, but it was at about this time that it joined the Cinque Ports as a corporate Member of Dover. As with much of the Confederation's expansion, the reasons for its joining are conjectural; it was untouched by cross-channel raiding, and this, together with its discrete economic stability, must have made it an attractive suitor; the town too, would have welcomed the growing influence of the Ports in its dealings with the monastic estates, and additional protection from the growing piracy in the Thames estuary and the channel.

The coast had stabilised by the thirteenth century and land reclamation commenced around the Swale, with the inevitable slowing of tidal scouring of the creek which has ever since suffered problems of silting. Whilst this must have inhibited its expansion as a trading port, it still grew on the strength of its agricultural surpluses; the importance of its maritime industry is shown by the town seal of around 1200, which shows a crude 'hulk', the ubiquitous broad-beamed load-carrier of medieval time.

The town continued to attract royal attention, with Henry II granting a charter to the Abbey to hold a fair. In 1252, Henry III confirmed the town's privileges as a Corporation from 'time immemorial', and referred to the Freemen of the town as Barons, a title equating with those of the Cinque Ports. There were several other charters granted subsequently, but none of present significance, except in the ceremonial right of the mayor to have a mace-bearer. The charter of 1260, which was the first to the Cinque Ports collectively, was that upon which the town's administration was based under the Mayor and twelve Jurats, who were Justices of the Peace; they enjoyed a wide-ranging jurisdiction over numerous offences, in common with many other towns, but their membership of the Cinque Ports extended their jurisdiction to capital offences; in early times, the right of appeal was to the Shepway but later this passed to the county assizes. The freemen were central to the town's affairs, and among their duties was the appointment of wardens to check for over-pricing, under-weighting, and ensuring that merchandise was 'fit for purpose'.

That Faversham was playing its part in the defensive role of the Ports, is indicated by the thirteenth century corporate seal showing a ship at war with three sailors, captain, five soldiers and two trumpeters; unusually, instead of the arms of the Cinque Ports, the shield shows the cross of St

George and, on the reverse, the legend 'I am the King's Port'. Faversham therefore, whilst acknowledging its membership of the Ports by enjoying its wide jurisdiction and providing its ship service, nevertheless maintained a greater degree of independence than other Members. The independence was insufficient to curtail the demands of the Lord Warden however, to whom the town was giving over 1,000 fish per annum, and which had risen to 2,000 herring and 100 salt fish by 1446.

In 1282 King Edward I commanded the town to support him in the Welsh campaign and, in 1296, Ports were summonsed to serve in the Scottish campaign; Faversham is recorded as having provided the *Nicholas* with thirty-four men. Their membership of the Ports was more restrained than some, but nevertheless in 1320 a Faversham ship pirated one of Newcastle, and received a strong protest accordingly. In 1322, the Ports were required to make ready with double equipment against a threatened invasion from France; the Faversham Barons were enjoined to keep watch over the activities of the Count Eustace of Flanders, and accordingly provided the *Barge*. The Faversham fleet at that stage was not large because, in 1337, the town found it necessary to hire *La Katerine* for the King's service at the opening of the Hundred Years' War; ten years later, when the siege of Calais employed a total of 100 ships and 14,151 men, the town's contingent comprised only two ships and 35 men.

The town's population in 1327 had grown to around 1,000, but a comparison of this with the recorded number of ships suggests that fishing and water transport were not its major activities, which were agriculture and brewing, and led to the establishment of the wool market in 1389. The scale of the fishing is illustrated by the nature of the numerous small fish weirs constructed from early in the century, together with eel trapping, and shore walking through the shallows for flat fish; this was a very different approach from the fleets of the other Ports, but it was nevertheless sufficient to warrant their appearance at Yarmouth.

By agreement with Dover, the town later nominated one of its Barons to serve in every third Parliament; by 1438, in addition to ship money, Faversham was paying Dover an annual rent of 40s for the election of a Baron as one of the Dover representatives. The town also played its part in the history of the Ports, with the continuous service given by Henry Pay, who was rewarded by being made admiral of the fleet, and was much feared by the French and Spanish. He is noteworthy for having inflicted defeat on the French near Milford Haven in 1405, and for having crushed a French merchant fleet with the capture of 120 ships in 1407; he died in 1419 and is buried in the parish church.

The sixteenth century saw few changes in the town's fortunes, other than of a steady progress which merited the 1520 pictorial map of the of the creek entrance showing its beacon. The town continued to find favour with the hierarchy, both ecclesiastical and political; in 1516, the Lord Warden, then Lord Abergavenny, and the Lords Chief Justice sat at Faversham, and the Archbishop of Canterbury made many visits; in 1519 Henry VIII and Catherine came, accompanied by Cardinal Wolsey; in 1521 Henry VIII and the Emperor Charles V stopped there on passing through, and in 1526 Cardinal Wolsey was again at Faversham in the year in which Henry resolved on his first divorce.

Almost to the eve of the Reformation, the Abbey was still in the favour of Henry who granted it a charter to hold a second fair and, in 1537, the Grammar School was first endowed. In 1538, the Abbey estates were surrendered to the King, the Abbot was pensioned off, and the Grammar School disappeared; following the dissolution, the town received its great charter of 1546 restating its administrative structure, and passing to it all the rights of the Abbey. At this time, Thomas Cheney was in the Crown Office dealing with the redistribution of ecclesiastical assets and received, with much more, the revenues of the Abbey; he was knighted and appointed Lord Warden, together with the post of Commissioner of Customs for the Port of Faversham.

His protégé, Thomas Arden, became Mayor in 1547 and took up residence in the Abbey guesthouse in Abbey Street; he was acquisitive by nature and, in 1549, he had the Fair moved to his own lands and took the profit, as a result of which he was deposed; he was later murdered by his unfaithful wife and her accomplices.

The Abbey Gatehouse and Arden's House

The Abbey was undoubtedly a place of beauty, and an elaborate spiritual institution that Stephen had intended as a royal mausoleum, but the buildings were raided and the stone used for the paving of Court Street that was constructed of extra width to accommodate the markets. In 1559, the first sluice on the creek was built to enable tidal flushing of the waterway. The Market Hall that, in 1574, became the Guildhall with the fish market beneath followed it in 1560; then, the consumer preference was for freshwater fish, seawater fish being considered somewhat coarse with the important exceptions of oysters and other molluscs. By 1565 however, the harbour was in decline due to severe silting, and the town was down to much the same size as Dover, having only 380 houses and 18 ships. Improvements were effected and, by 1570, the port facilities included two storehouses to the wharf, and a crane, together with another storehouse and a fish market adjoining the Town Quay; this storehouse survives as a Sea Cadets' centre, and is now named the *T.S.Hazard* after the Faversham ship built to serve against the Spanish Armada. In 1583, a new town crane was ordered on the instructions of the benefactor Henry Hatch, whose enduring legacy is still applied to the management of the creek. It was only by the following year that the Thames estuary had been charted, showing many beacons and buoys.

Whilst silting was crippling many of the other Ports, and Sandwich in particular had ineffectually petitioned Queen Elizabeth I for support, Faversham was faring rather better because its port was at that time merely an adjunct to the agricultural activities.

Elizabeth was suitably impressed when she stopped there in 1572, because it was one of the few towns to have paved streets in the centre, and boasted the largest parish church in Kent; in 1576 she provided for the endowment of a Free Grammar School, the new School House of which was built in 1587, and still stands.

The Elizabethan Grammar School

Whilst the administration of many towns grew from merchant guilds, this was not the generally the case with the Cinque Ports because, in a sense, the Ports were a guild in themselves by virtue of their charters. Faversham however, had the Fraternity of Free Fishermen, working the oyster beds as tenants of the Abbey and, after the dissolution, this continued to play an importantly wider part in the town's administration; this was no guarantee of avoiding disputes because, late in the reign of Elizabeth and twice subsequently, no less than three surveys of the rights and boundaries of the oyster beds had been required!

When Cromwell came to power, the Abbey buildings were effectively razed; the storehouses at the rear of Standard Quay were among those built from salvaged materials, but the present attractive timber clad buildings on the frontage are of no historical significance. John Trowts of Faversham, a supporter of King Charles I, fled to Holland where he spent time at Brede with the future King Charles II; on the restoration of the monarchy, the town made him mayor and he was visited by Charles who, in the same year, appointed John Wilson of Abbey Street as the first Master of the King's Music.

One of the important sources of the town's revenue was the 'droits', traced back to as early as 1539, which were levied on all goods passing through the town, as distinct from goods landed; inevitably, serious disputes arose between the town and members of the other Ports, who claimed exemption by virtue of their all-embracing charters; this was settled in favour of the town, with the exception of coal which was left undecided. The town was served by licensed porters, a system dating from 1443 with a fixed tariff for almost every conceivable item, including conveyance between brewer and tapster; they also had the function of apprehending minor miscreants, executing the pillory and the ducking stool, and the breaking of bakers' ovens as punishment for short weight.

In the mid sixteenth century, the port of Faversham was thriving. In 1574 the town, with the assistance of its rural parishes, erected the Market Hall with the sundial at its southeast corner, and the pillory at the northeast. A 1566 list of Kent shipping showed Dover as ranking first in the county with 20 ships averaging 34 tons, Sandwich with 17 ships averaging 18 tons, and followed by Faversham with 28 ships averaging 10 tons; this is consistent with Faversham's trade remaining predominantly coastal and, by 1629, it was still pre-eminent in the coastal trade with London, with 30 ships averaging 11 tons; Dover, Sandwich and Margate however, all had the larger fleets.

London, as a port, was growing rapidly, but the nature of Faversham's trade was enhanced rather than diminished by this. The London fishmongers, as well as buying from the masters of the Faversham fishing boats, were also operating their own, and the Faversham Port Book of 1580 records that the London fishmongers owned all cargoes of fish. The town's competitiveness was also enhanced by its unique practice of no ship having a permanent master or crew, with all being on standby; not only this, but at one time, of the 123 listed sailors, sixty were apprentices who were required to work unpaid for three years before listing as a sailor. The latter part of the century saw the Faversham fishermen complaining bitterly of domination of the waters by the French and Dutch fleets, at the small net sizes which they used, and their aggressive tactics in English home waters; even their complaint of potential enemies gaining knowledge of the waters was of no avail. The naval defences at the time were unable to respond, and the local fishermen were reduced to continuing reliance on a multitude of fish weirs, notwithstanding the danger these presented to inshore navigation.

The threat of invasion was growing. In 1587 the threat was from the Dunkirkers under the Duke of Parma; Faversham had resolved to contribute to the defence, but the threat failed to materialise. In the following year, the Guestling heard claims between Dover and Faversham as to the allocation of ship service, with Faversham's wish to contribute in its own right being allowed; the *Hazard* of forty tons was prepared and, in 1596, the town contributed another ship to reinforce the fleet harassing the Spanish coast.

At the end of the century, there were the combined issues of the need for regulations to conserve fish stocks, and to expand local adminis-tration into the vacuum left by the declining authority of the Cinque Ports. The Free Fishermen who had been working the oyster beds as tenants, but in fact fished for anything, were one of the few organised associations; initially therefore, the Oyster Fishery rules were extended to cover the trout and salmon seasons, the salmon being a commercial catch in the Medway until as late as 1833. There were also the Water Courts, the 1599 Folios of which disclose a variety of rules covering such matters as the procedure on the finding of dead bodies and the provision for their burial, the ownership of wreck in the Swale, the disposal of flotsam jetsam and lagons, and smuggling; they also provided for self-policing by the oyster fishermen, including severe penalties for forestalling and regrating. In 1614, the Faversham Mercers Company was formed, requiring all traders to be members and subject to the Corporation's bye laws; the freedom to trade within the town was extended to other members of the Cinque Ports, too.

In the seventeenth century the town had two market days, plus a daily fish market, and the wool market was still flourishing; originally, the market was only for local traders, but was subsequently opened to 'foreigners'. It was still an important coastal trading port for a variety of goods, including corn, flour, hops, malt, wool, leather, timber and fish; there was the important export of gunpowder, and of copperas stone to Brightlingsea. Early in the century, Faversham had the largest volume of shipping in the county at 2,063 tons and, by the end of the century this had grown to 2,800 tons but with only seven ships registered at the port; this was reflected in the volume of wool exports which in 1662 had amounted to 568 sacks, rising to 2,499 in 1699, before falling to 1,714 in 1712-13; even at that date, it was more than all the other Kent ports combined. This busy coastal trade backed by a productive agricultural hinterland, encour-aged the founding of Shepherd Neame's brewery in 1698, and it is still a serious contender in the brewing stakes. Until the 1980's, Faversham also boasted two other breweries.

The arrangement for collecting customs dues around the country was simplified by having a number of Head Ports, through whom all dues were collected. Faversham was one of these, whose responsibilities ex-tended through Whitstable, Reculver, and Margate to the North Foreland; in 1676, it was a fully fledged Port with both Town and Standard being legal Quays, although it enjoyed relatively little overseas trade when compared with its coastal trade; in 1683 London was still importing around six cargoes a week from Faversham, more than from any other Kent port except Whitstable.

The 1685 Edict of Nantes in saw many leaving the continent to escape religious persecution and settling in the towns of Kent, bringing with them a variety of industries. In Faversham, the industries of particular importance were tanning and the making of leather goods; the importance of leatherwork in those days cannot be underestimated, because it was used not only for clothing but also for a variety of commercial and industrial purposes, including lining the gunpowder punts - it was the polythene sheet of the day.

In 1688 William of Orange was invited to overthrow King James II and ascend the English throne, to inhibit the return of Catholicism to England. James fled, but was captured unrecognised at the Isle of Sheppey by a Faversham force and brought back to the town; inevitably, he was then recognised and detained at a house in Market Place, but was subsequently allowed to return to Westminster from where he went into exile.

The opening of eighteenth century saw a general downturn in the town's fortunes, which coincided with the arrival of the Hanoverians. In 1700, the decline in oyster stocks brought about a ban on trading with the Dutch who had been taking vast quantities. By 1703 the creek had also become inaccessible to the larger vessels, a condition which was to last some twenty-five years, although the fruit trade with London still continued; the creek sluice was also detrimental to the working of the mills, and was too small to permit the passage of the larger barges to the upstream quays.

Although these were difficult times, with the country being almost continuously at war and with threatened revolts at home, the town was positioned to prosper. 1716 saw establishment of the charity schools which were to last some 137 years, and 1725 saw the rebuilding of the upper floor of the Market Hall as a meeting room and store for weights and measures, from which time it became the Guildhall. In 1736 the manufacture of gunpowder was of sufficient importance for the £800 cost of rebuilding the creek sluice to be shared between the Corporation and the Ordnance Board, the previous sluice no longer being large enough to allow the passage of the larger barges to the upstream quays. The political uncertainties made it expedient for the government to buy out the gunpowder mills between 1745 and 1759, but the cash injection into the town enabled the new corn exchange to be built in 1750, by which time it was customary to sell on sample rather than bringing the whole shipment to auction; it was also from this time, that the weekly markets went into decline with emergence of a new breed of shopkeepers.

There was some further prosperity in the latter part of the century, with Edward Jacob commencing the Faversham Oyster Fishery in 1774, and this was possibly the earliest company in the world; the company's later warehouse of Victorian times still stands on Standard Quay, now skilfully converted into offices. At that time, whilst periodic sluicing of the creek was still a tolerably effective method of clearance, even more so was the laborious raking organised by the Corporation; a tax was levied on every owner of a vessel of over seventy tons at the rate of a man with a shovel and rake to work six days a year, with the owners of smaller vessels being taxed at half rate. There was sufficient shipping in the late eighteenth century for Trinity House to take an active interest in the local navigation, with many landmarks being shown on the north Kent coast, and the showing of the buoyage at the entrances to the Swale and Faversham Creek on a chart of 1786.

The shipping of gunpowder through the town was causing justifiable concern as, by that time, there were three factories and there had been several small explosions. In 1786 therefore, the works were relocated into the marshes, with a scattering of stores, mills and magazines, served by a network of canals; the materials were transported in wooden punts, leather lined, and with all fittings in bronze, but there were continual difficulties in keeping the waterways clear. In the mid 1700's, the mills reverted to private ownership under John Hall and, in 1920, became a part of Nobel Industries and were the largest site in the country; in 1926, under ICI Ltd, the works were closed and manufacture consolidated elsewhere. The marshland site remains, extending some 800m on the western side of the town, although much has been destroyed by gavel working; there remain the partly restored Chart Mills, which were among the earliest, on the northern side of the town at the head of Ospringe Creek.

In 1778 the simultaneous confrontations with France, Spain and the Americas, stimulated the formation of the Company of the Cinque Ports Volunteers, but it was not called for and was therefore disbanded, only to be reformed in 1794 to counter the Napoleonic threat; it was disbanded in 1800, and reformed again in 1803 with two companies from the town. The defence was readied for the threatened invasion from Boulogne, which did not materialise, and the Company was finally disbanded in 1810.

At the end of the century, the wool trade had declined to about one-half of its peak levels, and the oyster fisheries were severely damaged by the great frost of 1793. Within five years, the town had much improved the navigation, with the quays again accessible to vessels of eighty tons' burden and, on spring tides, with as much as eight feet draught. In those days the ships were mostly hauled up the creek by hand for the three miles from Hollow Shore; with way on, this was not as arduous an undertaking as might be supposed and the real skill was in maintaining direction. There were too, some fourteen lighters owned by the Corporation to bring the cargoes up to the quays, whilst some of the smaller vessels 'drudged' with the tide.

In 1801, the population had climbed to 3,364, with 578 houses; by 1831, this had grown further to 3,982 with 737 houses; this was not a particularly impressive growth, but the lower occupancy rate of the houses suggests a growing wealth in the town, although a contemporary survey noted little industry of significance; this was notwithstanding the six brick works supplying the expansion of London, and the two breweries; the brickworks were not to last long however, as the brick clay was soon exhausted and only one works remains.

The mid nineteenth century was a period of local government reform, much overdue with numerous town corporations enjoying varying degrees of autonomy, to say nothing of the anomalous status of the Cinque Ports and their members. An enquiry at Faversham noted that there was no manufacture in the town other than for a small cement works and a few powder mills, and that its economy was generally static following the closure of the government mills; it was also noted that there were large imports of amounting to 16,000 - 17,000 tons per annum, of which some two-thirds were carried inland; there were still substantial imports of timber from the Baltic, much of which was destined for Canterbury, but elsewhere inland too, and the town's exports were mainly of agricultural produce. Whatever the underlying economic growth rate might have been, Faversham clearly remained an important distribution centre at a time when sailing barges were still heavily in use; the Corporation applied itself to improvements of the creek, including hand cutting a new course to reduce the final bends. The Municipal Corporations Act of 1835, brought the long-standing local administration into line with the rest of the country.

In 1846, the high explosive guncotton was discovered, and manufacture commenced in Faversham in the same year, but closed in the following year as a result of an explosion in which eighteen staff died; the works reopened in 1873, and expanded into making an extensive range of pyrotechnical products. In 1900, the town's economic growth halted with the merger of the cement works with those on the Medway; this, together with the ending of the brickworks, had a disastrous effect on the navigability of the creek, with little further traffic and the need for dredging. The one small consolation in 1905, was the discovery in the town of the text of the 1260 charter of Henry III.

The gunpowder works responded to the onset of the First World War, with an expansion of the workings to cover some 500 acres. In 1916, at lunchtime on April 2, a fire caused by the careless storage of materials caused a major explosion and triggered two more in rapid succession; there were over 100 fatalities and sixty six injuries, and the force was sufficient to be heard as far away as London, Norwich, and France; many of the dead are buried in a mass grave in St Mary's churchyard.

There had always been some shipbuilding in Faversham, mostly to supply the town's own demand; at one time there was a yard operating in Creek Basin, and another at Goldfinches' Yard at the end of Standard Quay, but these businesses fell away with the demise of the sailing barges. In 1914, James Pollock and Sons Ltd took over one of the defunct brickyards with its quay on the west bank, and commenced the building of commercial and naval vessels, including the earliest of the ferro-concrete ships. The yard was very successful in vessels generally of up to 120ft overall, which were launched sideways into the creek; notable orders completed were for the 1958 *Ulco* bulk petroleum carrier, the 1965 *Broadness* salvage vessel later used in the recovery of the *Marchioness* after the Thames tragedy in 1989, and the 1973 launch of the deep sea trawler *Duffies III*. In 1972, the yard was taken over by Southern Shipbuilders [London] Ltd, but which went into liquidation in 1976. The site was subsequently occupied as a small industrial estate, with the waterfront nowdeveloped for housing; the small slipway between the two terraces is the only reminder of the past.

Today, Iron Wharf occupies an extensive railway marshalling yard of the inter-war era, and Standard Quay maintains the handful of permanently berthed classic barges providing a picturesque setting at high water; at the head of the creek, the Town Quay is backed by the green and the T.S.*Hazard*, with the Victorian sluice beyond. The town centre, a few minutes walk away via Abbey Street, is as unspoiled as any.

Around and About

A walk through the town must be a priority, and a call at the *Fleur de Lys* information centre in Preston Street will reward with a wealth of information including pamphlets describing the town walks and events; an excellent Town Guide is also available from the Council offices 50m uphill. These are best digested at the Sun Inn in West Street, where it is quiet in the daytime. On Saturdays in the summer season, there is a guided tour leaving the centre at 10.30hrs, for which booking is advisable; the centre's pamphlets are excellent.

From Iron Wharf, a turn up alongside the creek passes the 1845 Oyster Company warehouse, thence *via* Standard Quay where the barges are best seen near high water, and behind which is a delightful collection of eighteenth century stores built from materials salvaged from the Abbey. A continuation behind the creek via Belvedere Road leads into Conduit Street, off which is Bridge Street housing the early sluice gate immediately above the Town Quay with its green, and the T.S.*Hazard* built as a town warehouse in 1475.

A right turn right into West Street, over Tanners Street, and immediately left into the Westbrook Walk alongside the mill stream, leads to the partly-restored Chart Mills gunpowder works; these are usually open from 10.00 hrs to 16.00 hrs on summer Saturdays, but not in June. An exit via the footpath into Lower Road, a left *via* South Road and a left again into Tanners Street, leads to the Catholic Church and the national shrine to St Jude; the presbytery is a fine example of Georgian domestic architecture, but the church was a school before conversion to a cinema, only finding its present use in 1937; access to the shrine is from the rear of the interior.

T.S. *Hazard*   West Street

A return to South Road finds the magnificently elaborate Victorian alms-houses; from there, it is a short step to West Street, where the fifteenth century street scene includes the Sun Inn. The Ship Inn is no longer an inn, but the site of one since the sixteenth century; from there a right turn into Preston Street finds the *Fleur de Lys* information centre on the left, and leads naturally to the town museum; a short detour into Jacob's Yard and Gatefield Lane is worthwhile, and opposite is the house of Edward Jacob the eighteenth century mayor and historian.

At the corner with the spacious Court Street are the Guildhall and No 12 Market Street where James II was held. A return via East Street and down to the bottom of Church Road finds St Mary's church on the corner, with its ornate spire and fine interior dating from 1306.The footpath from the northwest corner passes the Elizabethan Grammar School building, and the adjoining Physic Garden; the Garden is on the site of the Abbey garden, and is now used appropriately for a mental health rehabilitation project.

The return to Abbey Street passes Arden House on the corner; originally, this was the inner gateway to the Abbey, and was later the home of Thomas Arden. Court Street otherwise has as good a collection of late medieval housing as you would wish for, and into which some modern development blends unusually well. From here, it is a short step back to the quays with refreshment opportunities on the way.

Court Street

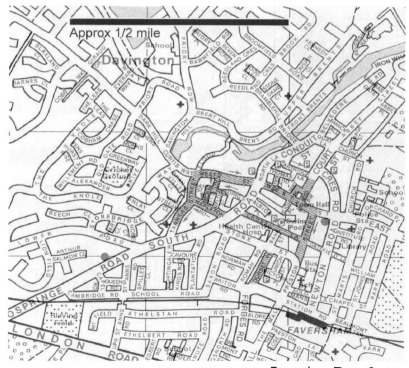

Faversham Town Centre

Rail		Faversham [3/4M] *[0845 748 4950]*
Buses		Kent C C Traveline *[0870 608 2608]*
Taxis		A1 5388867; Reeves [536666]; Starlight [24hrs] [591066]
Hospital	[A&E]	Canterbury *[01227 766877]*
	Cottage	Stone Street [562066]
Doctor		Faversham Health Centre, Bank St [562011]
Dentist	[NHS]	Hilton, Newton Place [591899]
Police		Church Road [not 24hrs] [477055]

Information Centre		Fleur de Lys, 13 Preston St [534542]
		www.faversham.org
Municipal Offices & Information		Alexander Centre, Preston St [594442]
Museum		Preston St
Churches	C of E	St Mary's, Church St [538334]
	R C	St Jude's, Tanners St [532449]
	Methodist / URC	Preston St [532461]

Shops	Numerous in town centre, but mostly small
Pharmacy	Preston St
Banks	Most are represented in the town centre

Public Houses	Numerous, including
	The Leading Light, Preston St [predictable Wetherspoons]
	The Sun Inn, West St [good food, quiet in the daytime]
	The Bear Inn, Market Place [reasonable food]
	The Phoenix Tavern, Abbey St [Thai & conventional food]
	The Anchor, Abbey St [reputedly top pub grub, not Mons]
Restaurants	Numerous cafes, but few licensed restaurants
	Shelley's, Market Place [traditional] [531750]
	China Village, Market Place [591288]
	India Royal, East St [536033]

Entertainment	Leisure Centre & Theatre, Bank St; Cinema, Market Place
Town Events [subject to confirmation]	Street Markets [Tues & Sat]
	Various 'open days' July & Aug
	Annual Smack & Barge Race in the Swale [first weekend in August]
	Raft Race, Funfair, Arts & Environment Fair [second weekend in August]

Notes:

Approximate Tidal Differences *[Spit]*	Sheerness -0hrs15; Dover +1hrs20
Charts	Admiralty SC2482; Imray 2100.3, Y14; Stanford 8
Weather	Iron Wharf [536296] [for customers]; Metcall [5 day] *[09068 500*
Navigation Authority	*455]*
	Medway Navigation Service [Ch16, 74 in the Medway] [663025]
Coastguard	Thames MRSC [signals on Ch16 are unreliable] *[01255 675518]*
Kingsferry Bridge	Ch 10 [423627]
	Clearances with bridge up/down 9m/34.4 above datum
	Depth 3.5 below datum

Yards	Alan Staley, Shipbuilders, Faversham [530668]
	slip, general repairs
	Testers, Hollow Shore [532317]
	crane, slip, berthing, general repairs, WC [showers]
	Young Boats, Oare [536176]
	crane, berthing, storage, general repairs
	chandlery, Calor, WC
	Iron Wharf, Faversham [536296]
	crane, tug, minor repairs, berthing & storage
	chandlery, marine diesel, water, [elec], WC, showers [£1 coin]
	laundromat

Fuel	Marine diesel from yards; petrol in cans from garages
Calor [No Gaz]	Young Boats
Chandlery	Iron Wharf [531777]

Repairs Elec & VHF	Swale Marine [Queenborough] [580930]
Spars & Rigging	Davis Marine, Military Rd, Ramsgate *[01843 586172]*
Sails	Wilkinson Sails, Conyer [521503]

Notes: Kingsferry Bridge lifts are currently curtailed [Summer 2005]

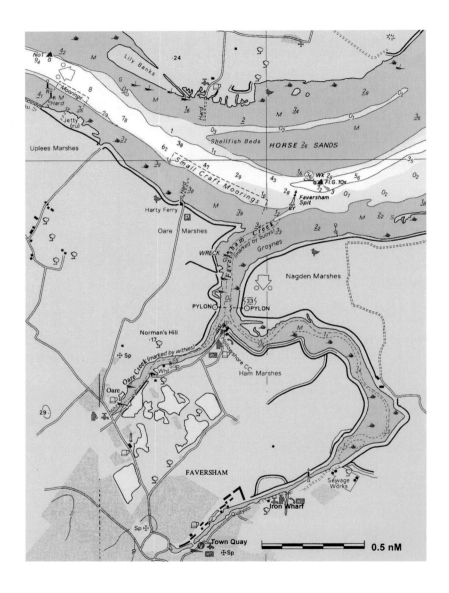

The Swale and Faversham Creek   Adapted from Admiralty 2482

Navigation and Berthing

The entrances to the Swale are well buoyed from both east and west; there is a significant volume of commercial traffic at the western end, and occasionally in the Swale itself taking the north channel at Fowley Island. The Kingsferry Bridge, with its lifting span between the two pairs of landmark towers, opens to order, but the road and rail traffic take clear precedence; the preferred procedure is to call on Ch10 [or 'phone 01795 423627] when about a mile off and request an opening time, or to approach and sound 1 long + 2 short blasts; it is otherwise necessary to approach and hoist a bucket or to otherwise make the intention obvious, but the bridge will not be lifted until your vessel is close to; in any event therefore, there is likely to be a mildly awkward wait stemming the tide and, as the bridge may not be fully lifted for a small craft, the green traffic signal may not be shown.

A new road bridge is under construction to the immediate west, and is due for completion in 2006. There are temporary navigational restrictions, and a bridge lift may not be available for leisure craft during peak periods; it is worth asking whether there is commercial traffic in the offing, and for which a lift will be provided.

The Swale is really two rivers, flowing east and west respectively, with the watershed at about Milton Creek. This causes an unusual tidal pattern, in that it floods from both ends but for the first hour or so of the ebb it flows eastwards; the watershed then moves eastwards from Long Point towards Fowley Island during the ebb and, in the vicinity of Faversham Spit, the spring ebb can run at over four knots; the charted depths should be treated with caution. In the absence of local knowledge throughout the Swale, it is better to keep to the well-buoyed channels. Having gained Faversham Spit, it is worth considering the berthing alternatives.

Off Faversham Spit, there is a useful anchorage to the immediate east of the Creek or in the blind north channel adjoining the Isle of Sheppey, and where there is good holding but little water; the visitors' buoys to the immediate west of the Spit are only suitable for craft displacing a ton or two, and the buoys upstream are private. A good dinghy and fine weather here provide the opportunity to land on the causeway of the long discontinued Harty Ferry, and explore the Oare Nature Reserve for a couple of hours; on the opposite bank is the sixteenth century Ferry Inn, with its extensive garden terrace, good food, B&B with *en suite* facilities, and showers for visiting yachtsmen are in hand, but booking is recommended [01795 510214]. Indeed, from here and armed with a robust outboard, Faversham's Town Quay is within an hour and would enable a short exploration of the town centre.

Entrance to the Creek should not be attempted at night or in conditions of poor visibility without local familiarity. At the Spit, the general rule is that when there is sufficient water there on a rising tide, there will be sufficient to make the head of the creeks if a prompt start is made; this may not hold true on full neaps, particularly for Oare Creek. An ample depth is found in the transit between the outer green buoy *Reflection* and *Faversham Spit* north cardinal, treating the latter as a starboard-hand buoy to provide alignment for the creek itself; a compass course is unhelpful, because the green buoy moves with the tide.

On entering the creek, the channel is well buoyed; the second starboard-hand marker should be given a wide berth, as it is set on a wreck which projects perhaps a boat's length into the channel; the cluster of sheds and masts on that hand indicates Tester's Hollow Shore Yard on Oare Creek. The entrance to Oare Creek is not marked; it is necessary to continue for some 50m upstream from the centre of the overhead power cables before turning in, and negotiating a short port hand bend before the creek straightens, as a direct course leads over the drying mud flats; there are numerous keel tracks in the mud to prove the point.

Beware!

Oare Creek offers berthing at Hollow Shore Yard, which continues some 200m upstream to a permanently moored barge; it specialises in the restoration of classic smacks, and many of these are raced. The yard caters mostly for permanent customers, with no alongside berthing, and it may be necessary to find an end-on mud berth temporarily vacant between the timber piles; there is water for about one hour either side of mean high water, and for only about half-tide by dinghy if mud-berthed off. If arriving out of office hours, it is sufficient to report to the Shipwright's Arms nearby, which provides showers for visiting yachtsmen and good food other than on Mondays and Tuesdays.

Above Hollow Shore there is a long continuation of private berths, before a staging and ivy-covered Dutch barn on the port hand marks the commencement of Young Boats; it is permissible for visitors to use this staging if there is insufficient water to proceed further. Above the barn, the channel is marked by withies for the next half-mile, when the visitors' berthing is to be found on the first starboard-hand pontoon; there is water here for about an hour at the top of most tides, but it is possible to be neaped.

The real disadvantage of these yards for the short-term visitor is that they are both a good thirty minutes' walk from the town centre. The footpath from Hollow Shore is across the fields, whilst that from Young Boats is via the roadway; both are accessible by taxi.

Faversham Creek itself winds some three miles through a pastoral setting that has changed little over the centuries. The channel is adequately buoyed for the whole length but must be followed with care; the deepest water is to be found in the centre of the channel on the straight sections, and otherwise at the apex of the bends, but the depth is not uniform; there is a couple of shallows, but passaging on a rising tide will find sufficient water. If grounded, Iron Wharf will be helpful during working hours.

Iron Wharf   Town Quay

The commencement of Iron Wharf is marked by a line of private staging on the port hand, followed by an old steel barge used as a dry dock; here, the best water is found immediately above the barge for better than one hour either side of mean high water. Nearing the top of tide, there are increasing back eddies against the wharf which extend progressively to mid stream until merging with the downstream flow, and these can be a useful aid to manoeuvring; berthing is on the soft mud bank adjoining the quay and rafting up is the norm, but the concreted standing beneath the mobile crane should be left clear. On berthing, it is vital to set shore lines and springs, and to take an access ladder from the quayside, all having regard to the 2.5m tidal range; fender boards and ample fenders are recommended, as is the removal of outboard deck gear at risk from adjoining shore lines. The yard is informal and is there for those who enjoy their boats; advance notice is appreciated, but casual berthing is almost always available; it is about a half-mile from the town centre.

Upstream, there are the small yards of Alan Staley, and Standard Quay beyond with its barges; these have no visitors' berths. At the head of the creek, immediately below the bridge and sluice, there is private staging on the starboard hand, and the Town Quay on the port hand immediately below the bridge, with ample space to turn; there is about a metre here at low water, which is more than in the creek generally, and this should be borne in mind when planning departure. The quay was refurbished in 1988 with adequate bollards and fixed ladder access, but the only other facility is a cold water tap, and there is no security; it does have the advantages of being free of charge for a short stay, and being only a quarter-mile from the town centre.

Brightlingsea in Bloom

'Brightlingsea in Bloom' was founded in 1994 to commemorate the fifty years of peace in 1995, and has continued since with the able support of dedicated volunteers; in 1998, the town was the 'Runner Up' in the national competition. This picture was taken from near the 1250 All Saints Church on the hilltop above the town.

BRIGHTLINGSEA

BRIGHTLINGSEA is not as obviously attractive as many ports and harbours, but a better acquaintanceship is well worthwhile. It has enjoyed close links with the Cinque Ports since the fifteenth century; it still retains a strong maritime flavour, and its real advantage for the visiting yachtsman is, as it has been for centuries, the provision of the most convenient good shelter between the north Kent and east coasts. The town is unpretentious, but has adequate facilities and is very welcoming; it is a popular berthing, dinghy sailing and caravanning centre, and is otherwise a dormitory for Colchester.

History

The area has been occupied since the Bronze Age, and was settled by the Celtic *Trinobantes*, on whom the Roman occupation made little impact. It was then attacked and settled by the Danes, and the original *Britric's Land* shown on a sixteenth century map reflects its Anglo-Saxon origins; it is otherwise the *Britriceseia* of the Domesday Book and, later, *Brickelsey*. The early town is on the elevated ground above what was the harbour marshland, and the single road towards Colchester is still the essential access; the scattered nature of the early agricultural communities is reflected in the thirteenth century Parish Church of All Saints being situated some two miles inland; the oyster and fishing industries, now depleted, date from Roman times with a continuously uneasy relationship with the big sister, Colchester.

The entry in the Domesday Book noted that '*... Britriceseia was held by Harold as a manor and as ten hides. Now King William ...*' and, by 1096, it was in the hands of Eudo de Rice, William's favourite steward. De Rice remained in favour with both William II and Edward I; he founded the Abbey of St. John the Baptist at Colchester and gave it the manor of Brightlingsea, as was confirmed by the charter of William II; he experienced difficulties with the monks, retook the manor but later re-granted it.

The grant included a wide jurisdiction; there was remitted the *soc and sac* and *ingangtheof*, together with the proceeds of many fines and extensive hunting rights; these rights were, in parts, distributed among other ecclesiastical establishments, including St. Mary's Colchester and the

St. Osyth Priory. The seminal grant was important, although by no means unusual in nature, and it was far less embracing than those to the Cinque Ports. Brightlingsea must have assumed a much earlier importance however, because it had been recognised by Harold and, as an ancient demesne, it enjoyed extensive privileges; these included avoidance of some of the harsher impositions of the feudal system, recourse to the royal courts, freedom from tolls in all markets and customs houses, and from enforced attendance at the Shire Court. This degree of independence, reinforced by its geographical isolation, quickly led to friction with both the Abbey and with the town of Colchester.

The port was proving a valuable asset to the ecclesiastical demesnes, who themselves were experiencing friction with that at Colchester; it was a landing place for vast quantities of fish, and was convenient also for the export of sheep; the town evidently had a share in the regional wealth, because it merited the very substantial Parish Church of All Saints, built in around 1250. The port also boasted a large fleet, profiting from Edward's wars; in 1299, the *Welfare* carried provisions to the King's stores at Berwick, for which they were paid £4; at about that time, Brightlingsea and St. Osyth between them were certified as able to find a barge of '40 oars and 30 tons burthen', and the town provided four ships in support of the Scottish war in 1325. The town was no more above piracy than any of the Ports because, in 1342, their participation led to the forfeit of one of their demesnes; in the same year however, they sent four ships to Brittany for the French campaign, the contrary winds requiring a return passage of sixty days. In 1346, the town was ordered to send to Portsmouth all ships of thirty tons and more for the campaign at Crecy and, in 1347, it sent five ships and sixty-one men for the siege of Calais. The recorded total provision to Edward was 54 ships and 283 men, compared with Colchester's 12 ships and 239 men.

The economy was shaken when the Black Death reached Colchester in 1348; there is no record of its impact on Brightlingsea but, probably, it too lost between one third and one half of its population. The resulting shortage of labour had much the same effect there as elsewhere; there was the emancipation of many feudal villeins, together with the commutation of services for money; even the stipend of the priests was increased, it proved impossible to continue the exercise of all manorial rights; in 1353, Thomas Moveron was elected Abbot of St. Mary's Priory, and at some time between 1359 and 1361 was replaced, reputedly for releasing ecclesiastical rights to the Cinque Ports; Moveron's Farm, to the north of the town, is a reminder of his influence.

Brightlingsea probably joined the Ports at some time 1350; the minutes of the Brotherhood in 1442, when town was granted its own charter confirming its rights, made it clear that it had been a member for many years; The history is poorly recorded, but the inference is that to have remained under the domination of either the church or Colchester town would have proved stifling, that an attachment to Yarmouth would not have been an option because Yarmouth's interests lay in the North Sea, but conversely the Cinque Ports needed a safe haven on passage to Yarmouth, with the Black Death at Sandwich having left that town short of mariners to fulfil its ship service; the outcome was to prove invaluable to Sandwich because one its other members, Stonar, was finally washed away by floods in 1365. Brightlingsea's alliance was challenged, but in 1442 it obtained from Sandwich a copy of its 'Freedoms of the Ports' as granted 'from time immemorial'.

The town recovered well. In the fifteenth century, it was one of the recognised ports for the carriage of wool to London and its export to the continent; indeed, some of the earliest surviving houses in the country remain in the town's High Street, having escaped the turmoil of the Civil War. Its success was attributable to the diversity of its activities, both agricultural and maritime; it was not only a commercial and fishing port, and a long established oyster fishery, but it also benefited from its association with the Confederation. In 1489, the *Michael* was engaged in the expedition to Brittany and, in 1497, the *Thomas* to Berwick to quell an uprising, carrying two demi-curtowes - short guns, each weighing about 300lbs, and used for field artillery. By the 1530's, and again in the 1590's, the town followed the pattern of behaviour common to the Ports, and Sandwich was required to intervene on its behalf in a dispute with Newcastle.

The inshore passage along the Essex coast was probably much as it is now, and its importance is illustrated by the early appearance of navigational marks; by the end of the fifteenth century, the Spitway was marked and in 1542, a Show Beacon was erected where the Maplin light is now; in 1584, this and the Whitaker Beacon appeared on charts, together with other marks and soundings in the vicinity; a chart of 1590 also gives All Saints as a landmark. These were the early days for charts, and anything more than the smallest of scale would have been highly inaccurate. Brightlingsea, the only member of the Confederation beyond Sussex and Kent, and having been little exposed to the cross-channel raiding, was better able to weather the implications of King Henry VIII's naval programme than were the head Ports. For his new navy for the French and Scottish wars, he took some of the town's shipwrights for the building of the *Grace Dieu*, and pressed mariners into service between 1512 and 1513; the *Barbara of Brykelsey* appeared several times in the Navy Lists from 1512, probably having been purchased from a town merchant, as did the *Anne* of 45 tons, the *Julian* of 40 tons, and the *Maryflower* of 40 tons, all serving as transports; in the following year, there were the additions of the

Trinitie of Brykelsey of 70 tons, and the *Peter and Poll of Brykelsey* of 50 tons. There were several more impressed to bring the King's army back from France and, in 1519, the *Katryn Plesaunce* carried 500 planks to Chatham. In 1522, in yet further wars, the *Mary of Brykelsey* is recorded as having carried dried cod and, in 1524, the *Mare Galant of Brykelsey* carried 244 tons of malt from Barrow to Berwick, both for the armies.

The temporary cessation of hostilities was followed by an increase in maritime trade, which was matched by the number of shipwrecks. The granted rights to these were an important source of revenue, and soon the Cinque Ports, the Burgesses of Colchester, and the Lord of the Manor of Brightlingsea, were all laying claim to these and to the Admiralty jurisdiction in the Colne estuary, and each with the support of conflicting Royal grants. The status of the Lord Warden was held to take precedence, and his court was further busy in settling disputes arising from ships in collision. The trade also attracted the attention of pirates, problems with which were noted in 1535.

In 1538, there was again the threat of invasion. All males between the ages of sixteen and sixty were required to prepare for national defence, and the town contributed to the Horse of the Tendring Hundred; in the following year, the town was charged with watching the coast and tending the beacons. King Henry VIII made the Colne a naval station in 1543 and, to confuse the enemy, had taken down the two 'showe beacons' indicating the Swin; soon too, mariners from the town were again pressed into service and, in 1545, the town became an embarkation point some five hundred soldiers quartered there.

A return of vessels of more than 100 tons was called for in 1559, and Brightlingsea was the only port in Essex to qualify, with the *Barke* of 100 tons; the *Maryflower* was included, notwithstanding earlier records of her smaller tonnage, but this may have been a later vessel of the same name. A 1565 survey for the Port of Ipswich included '*... A landinge place at Brykelsey which is in the Queen's towne parcell of the Cinque Ports, which hath at all times been a landynge place as well to transport merchandizes into the partes beyond the Sea, as from porte to porte within the Realme, and so is mete to be contynued, And the same is a place mete for the building of the Queen's Majesties Shipps, and is distant from Ipswich x myles xxij myles, from Harwich x mjles xvj mjles, ffrom Colchester vj myles vj mjles ...*'; the distances compared those by sea and by land.

Evidently, Queen Elizabeth I had cause to take more notice of Brightlingsea than of Sandwich, for in 1570 there were arrested for her service the *Anne Galant* of 100 tons, the *Mary Grace* of 56 tons, the *Mary James* of 42 tons, the *Mary Edward* of 50 tons, the *Lyon* of 30 tons, and the *Martyn* of 36 tons; this was all in spite of the Cinque Ports being technically excused. By 1582, neither Colchester nor Brightlingsea had a vessel of 100 tons or more, and a 1586 survey occasioned by fears of the Spanish, showed only ten ships of between six and eighty tons; in these times, the town reverted to fishing as its major maritime source of income and, by 1597, the Lord Warden was considering its severance from the Ports, notwithstanding its service in the expedition to Cadiz in the previous year. The times remained troubled for, in 1630, the 'Dunkirker' pirates were making their presence felt; if it was not one source of aggression, it was another, for a Dutch fleet of fifty or sixty vessels anchored in the Gunfleet in 1667 and sought to land at St. Osyth with sheep stealing in mind, but were driven off with a couple of them being left aground.

Again, Brightlingsea survived on its diversity of enterprise with a combination of special industry, oyster farming, fishing, salving and smuggling, all well into the eighteenth century. The original Cinque Ports Wreck Warehouse proved too small and, in about 1760, it was removed to Sydney Street where the building still stands as the only surviving example in the country. The processing of 'copperas', a constituent of London clay, commenced at about this time; it was dredged by local smacks and processed into an effective treatment for sheep scab; with the growth of the cloth industry it was also in demand as the principal black dye, and the town was one of the only three places of manufacture, that continued until as late as 1840 off Copperas Road.

With the fears of a French invasion, trained volunteer forces were established. These included the 1797 Brightlingsea Company of 'Sea Fencibles' notwithstanding the need to continue their occupation as fishermen; this, by 1801, comprised 101 men, and was manning the floating batteries anchored off the Gunfleet to close three of the passages through the sands. The 1808 and 1821 Acts of Parliament confirmed the Lord Warden's jurisdiction over town's Cinque Port status.

The Colne estuary was known for its oyster beds from Roman times; it was never much centralised as an industry, being conducted from small private beds licensed or rented, and the extensive remains of which were clearly visible in Brightlingsea harbour into the late 1990's. Oyster farming was very much a foreshore occupation until the gluts of the late eighteenth century, when the price dropped so dramatically that oysters became the poor man's fare for many years, with the inevitable result of over-fishing to maintain turnover; by the early nineteenth century, the beds were all but fished out, and the larger oyster smacks were surviving on a combination of oyster piracy and the exploration of new grounds in distant and deeper waters. The industry recovered on the finding of fresh stocks and varieties in the channel; these were imported for restocking and home cultivation but, whilst most harbours cultivated their new stocks, in Brightlingsea there was the policy simply of growing them on for quick resale. The East Coast smacks were larger, faster, and more aggressive than many in the smaller harbours, and this brought about regulation over the channel waters with the Anglo-French protocol of 1843. Just as the copperas industry came to an end, the oyster industry took over as the town's mainstay, albeit on a more modest scale, but oysters thereafter remained an exclusive fare. The rapid urban expansion of the late nineteenth century occasioned widespread sewage pollution of oyster beds, and the town was one of the few to respond with the construction of treatment tanks, sited in Oyster Tank Road off the foot of New Street.

It was in this time of urban expansion, with the town thriving on a combination of the oyster farming, fishing and the shipbuilding industries, together with coastal trading, that the harbour marshlands were reclaimed for building. This was the time of the great infill between the High Street and Waterside; although a seemingly uninspiring quarter, a closer look reveals what must have been a well-balanced distribution of wealth, because it includes an unusually high proportion of small detached and semi-detached dwellings. The increase in population called for the construction of New Church just behind Victoria Place, when it was reported that over sixty percent of the townsfolk attended its opening in 1814; by 1834, with the old Parish Church of All Saints being over a mile away, there was the demand for the new Parish Church of St. James, which was built in the High Street.

In the 1840's, Brightlingsea became the popular yachting centre which it is today, but then the fishing hands laid-off in the summer were available as paid crew for yachts, a practice which continued into the 1930's. Whilst many of the contemporary yacht designs undoubtedly reflected those of the fishing boats, it is thought that in Brightlingsea the design of the new and faster fishing smacks owed much to that of the yachts; the smacks from this time were of around fifty tons, 65ft on the deck with a 25ft bowsprit, and manned by a crew of three to five; in 1848, there were 160 in the harbour and, by 1861, the number had risen to over 200. As well as the commercial coasters, there were numerous sailing barges operating locally, all carrying around 100 tons of cargo, and these are known as have passaged as far as Cornwall and the Rhine. It is the smaller smacks of around 35ft that are sailed today.

The local shipbuilding had hitherto been a dispersed foreshore industry but, in 1863, the new Aldous Shipyard was created behind what is now the commercial quay. This, and the James & Stone shipyard, were responsible for many of the classic racing yachts, together with the building of inshore sailing coasters and barges; at the end of the nineteenth century, with the demise of commercial sailing, the yards turned successfully to building more modern commercial vessels with most of their orders being obtained from the British colonies; when these gained independence in the 1960's, the order books dried up completely in the face of competition from the Far East, and the yards closed; in 1964, the town lost its railway connection too. In spite of this, the town's population almost doubled to nearly 8,000, and has remained something of a growing dormitory for Colchester.

The closure of the yards left the commercial quay with limited use, but it enjoyed notoriety with its involvement in the breaking of the coal miners' strike in 1984, and in the live animals' exports of 1995; its use has now fallen to a few movements a month, importing ballast and timber, and exporting scrap metal to Spain. There remains the adjacent dock for classic smacks, of which a handful are usually present, and annual barge races are also held in the vicinity. In 2001, Colchester town discontinued its own moorings' management, and the Brightlingsea Harbour Commissioners established as a Trust Port in 1923, became the authority for the Colne Estuary, thus turning the tables on the big sister.

Around and About

At Waterside, there are the Colne Yacht Club, a chandlery and the Harbour Office, and an ascent of Tower Street leads to the High Street. There, a right turn passes early houses including the fourteenth century Jacob's House with its external stairway and, further on, is the pretty setting of Hurst Green with a view over the creek but its pub is uninteresting. A return along the other side of the High Street passes numerous other early buildings, including The Swan which was renovated in Victorian times; across the road is the seventeenth century Brewer's Arms, which is best when not at its busiest; suitably refreshed, a few moments should be spared in the much loved Victorian church of St. James before reaching Victoria Place. Here, the detail of the few older buildings is mostly obscured but, in the vicinity, are the Information Office, two supermarkets, and the colourful little Museum; the museum merits an hour or so, but its restricted opening times seem to vary from year to year.

Hurst Green

The Brewers Arms

A return via Promenade Way passes the holiday camp with its boating lake and the old sea wall beyond, Oyster Tank Road and the Brightlingsea Sailing Club, and thence *via* Colne Road to regain Waterside, with a short detour to pass the Wreck Warehouse in Sidney Street which is the only remaining in the country.

The Wreck Warehouse

The Smack Dock

There is a sports centre attached to the school in Church Road at about one mile from Waterside, and the open air pool and leisure area off Promenade Way; a little further reaches All Saints Church in a lovely rural setting, and a building steeped in history with its unique fresco of tiles commemorating those lost at sea. For the energetic, there is also a five miles' circular nature trail from Bateman's Tower, incorporating the old sea wall and the wetlands designated as of international importance. A leaflet is available from the information centre.

St Osyth Creek

A dinghy and a decent outboard enable the 2nM excursion up the St. Osyth creek close to St. Osyth it-self. It is accessible for about two hours either side of high water, with landing at the private quay of the St. Osyth Boatyard. on the top of most tides, there is access for craft of shoal draught, and staging for an overnight stay by prior arrange-ment.

The yard is friendly and specialises in the maintenance of classic boats; there is the usual combination of those that will never float again, classics, and something of everything in between.

A sailing barge stationed there offers day trips in summer; nearby are the excellent Mill House tea rooms, and the highly recommended White Hart which is open all day in the season; the recreational lake with its own facilities is opposite. A half-mile walk up the hill leads to the village, passing the magnificent walls of the St. Osyth Priory [which is not open to the public], and thence to the village itself with its narrow streets and a generous scattering of late medieval buildings; for centuries, this was a busy trading port served by sailing barges.

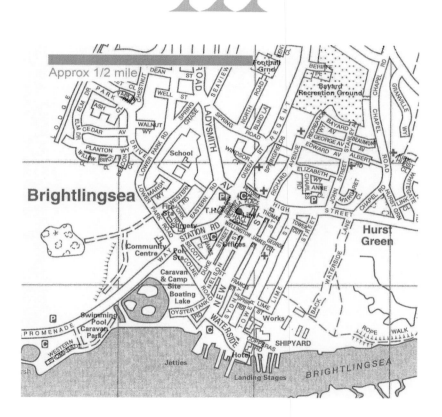

Brightlingsea Centre

Rail	Colchester North [inter-city] [91/2M] *[0845 748 4950]*
	Colchester Town [local] [9M] *[0845 748 0950]*
Buses Victoria Place:	Essex C.C. 'Traveline' *[08547 000333]*
Taxis	Brightlingsea Cabs [305006] Cedric's Coaches [824363]
Hospital [A&E]	Colchester [747474]
Doctor	Colne Medical Centre, Station Road [302522] [305235 out of hours]
Dentist	Piers Lambert, 53 Ladysmith Avenue [302307]
Police Station	Station Road [not 24hrs] *[01255 221312]*
	Marine Police, Burnham on Crouch [not 24hrs] *[01621 785961]*
Information Centre	Victoria Place [restricted hours] [303535]
	www.brightlingsea-town.co.uk
Museum	Duke Street [irregular hours]
Churches CofE	All Saints, High Street [302407/302378]
RC	St Sabina, Edward Ave [off Richard Ave] [302485]
Methodist/URC	Hurst Green [302170]
Banks	High Street and Victoria Place
Pharmacy	Victoria Place
Shops	Various small shops in High Street
Supermarkets	Spar & PO [Victoria Place]; Pioneer [Station Road]
Public Houses	Numerous of similar ambience, but few serving evening meals,
	The Brewers Arms [High Street]
Restaurants	Colne Yacht Club, Waterside [in season] [302594]
	Kevalan Restaurant, Waterside [Indian] [305555]
	Brightlingsea Chinese Restaurant, 56 High Street [303466]
	The Waterside Fish & Chip, Waterside [302710]
Entertainment	Sports Centre, Church Road
	Beach and Open-air pool, Promenade Way
Town Events [subject to confirmation]	Brightlingsea Carnival [June]
	Classic Barge and Smack Races [September]

Notes: There is a decently useful Take-Away Fish and Chips behind the Harbour Office [Tel 305377]

Approximate Tidal Differences	Harwich +0hr20
Charts	Admiralty SC3741; Imray 2000.7; Stanford 4
Weather	Local [751111 + 8325 at the prompt]; Metcall [5 day] [0968 500 455]
Coastguard	Thames Coastguard Ch16, 67; Walton-on-the-Naze *[01256 6755181]*
Navigation Authority	Brightlingsea Harbour Commissioners
Harbour Master	Ch 68; Waterside [302200]
Water Taxi	Ch37; *[07733 078503]*
Clubs	Colne Yacht Club, Waterside [302594]
	bar, meals in season, WC / showers, dinghy park, refuse bins
	[if closed, shower key from HM in office hours]
	Brightlingsea Sailing Club, off Colne Rd [302676]
Refuse	Colne Yacht Club [bins in dinghy park]
Pump-out	Pontoon, on application to HM
Fuel	French Marine, Waterside [petrol & road diesel in cans]
Calor & Gaz	French Marine, Waterside [Gaz]; Brightlingsea Boatyard [Calor]
Water	Standpipe on main slip
Chandlers	French Marine, Waterside; Brightlingsea Boatyard
Yards	Brightlingsea Boatyard, Waterside [upstream from Quay] [302003]
	tug, hoist, limited mud berthing, storage, limited repairs,
	outboards and inflatables
	St Osyth Boatyard, St Osyth *[01255 820005]*
	slip, limited berthing, general repairs
Engineer	French Marine Motors, Waterside [302133 / 305233]
Spars	Sailspar, Tower St [302679]
Sails	James Lawrence, Tower St [302863]

Notes: The Harbour Master and his Office are as helpful you could wish for.

Use their website for current conditions: www.brightlingsea.net/cam

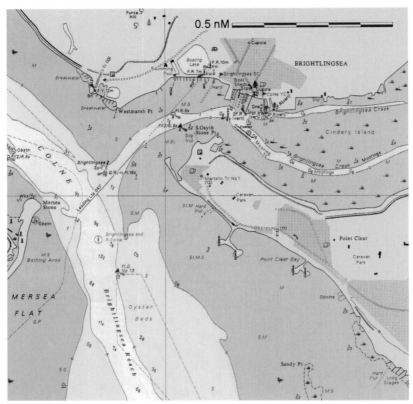

The Colne Estuary and
  Brightlingsea Creek

Adapted from Admiralty 3741

The buoyage in the Colne Estuary will always be open to revision!

Navigation and Berthing

The approach to Brightlingsea from the south-east is off the shore-line from St Osyth to Brightlingsea, and is recognisable by the extensive caravan parks; there is an 8kts speed limit extending a half-mile from the low water line and marked by a row of black plastic drums, and these also form a useful inshore navigation aid, although unlit. The Colne fairway is well buoyed, but the spit at St Osyth Point is growing; there is little water at buoys *Nos 9* [Fl.G] and *13* [Fl.G], and the centre of the channel should be favoured here; the buoyage in the vicinity will always be open to revision.

The approach from seaward is between Nos *10* [Fl.(2)R] and *13* [Fl.G], for the *Brightlingsea Spit* south cardinal [YB, Q(6)+LFl.15s]; the Spit is best avoided within 1 1/2 hrs of low water, as there is not the charted depth here, and it should be left to port within a boat's length at the most. The 1/12 tidal rule of thumb does not apply here, and wind over tide on a spring ebb can produce some very uncomfortable conditions.

From *Brightlingsea Spit*, the course is 041° T to pass between the port and starboard buoys [Fl.R.5s and F(3)G.5s] at about a 1/4m ahead, and a watch should be kept for any commercial traffic or dinghy racing; St Osyth's Stone Point to the east, is a landing area for water sports and speed boats whilst Mersea Stone, to the west, provides good anchorage off a steep-to shingle bank. Above the town is the spire of All Saints church and, below and a little to the right behind the beach huts and foreshore, are the leading marks; they are difficult to spot among a clutter of dinghy masts, and are only of help for entering if there is a strong cross-tide running; their red lights [R] are unreliable because of occasional vandalism.

The Entrance to Brightlingsea Creek

Having set course from the Spit, there is a speed limit of 4kts, and it really is worth while contacting the Harbour Master on Ch68 [or his office on 01206 302200]; if available, he is particularly helpful, notwithstanding his responsibility for the navigation marks up the River Colne, as well as maintaining the balance between the commercial and leisure uses of the harbour. The opportunity can be taken of asking whether there is any commercial traffic in the offing [normally only around high water], and where there is the best space on the pontoons. It is in order to ask for a friendly nudge into position whilst lines are secured, especially if short-handed in a bit of a breeze; quite probably, he will provide an escort if not too busy and, if the water taxi is not running, he will also provide a lift ashore.

From 50m beyond the red and green buoys, the course entails making a slow turn to starboard. As it progresses, the view of the harbour opens out along the front, past the defunct shipyard [soon to be redeveloped], the public slipway, the Edwardian chalet style public house [now flats], the incongruously modern clubhouse of the Colne Yacht Club with its jetty and, further to the east, the commercial quay; at the nearer end of this quay, there is a green-painted wall of stacked containers, and the approach entails wearing gently wear round and aiming at their seaward end, until the north cardinal [BY] near the end of the visitors' pontoon is identified. It is better not to stray inshore until the harbour has been seen at low water, because there is a long spit extending from Cindery Island between the waterside and the inshore trots.

The main pontoon is in two lengths between two lines of trots; the nearer length is usually occupied by larger vessels, and carries the pump-out facility. The tide runs parallel at up to 2kts, but there is not a lot of room to turn between the landward trots and the pontoon, and even less on the seaward side; there is more room at the further end, with 1m or so of water at MLWS.

The pontoons are modern, with ample cleats, but no other facilities; rafting up is the norm, and it is sensible to leave fenders out; shore lines and springs are required. The tapered finger at the western end of the inshore pontoon is reserved to the Harbour Master and the water taxi.

These are island pontoons. Shore access by dinghy offers the options of the town slip which is slippery and where the tidal state needs to be borne in mind or, alternatively, the Colne Yacht Club jetty available freely to members of the home and other clubs - but a dinghy left there should be taken to the back of the hammerhead to leave it clear for traffic. The water taxi also operates from there on Ch37 [or 07733 078503] during weekends in season, or otherwise by arrangement.

There is some berthing at the Brightlingsea Boatyard immediately upstream of the commercial quay, but this is tidal and of uncertain availability for the short-term visitor.

On leaving this well sheltered harbour it is worth remembering that, firstly, weather conditions outside will be at least a notch higher than inside and, secondly, that the leading marks are a useful back bearing when a strong outgoing tide holds the red buoy uncomfortably close to the shallows.

Hastings: The Net Houses and the Fishermen's Church Museum

The Net Houses stand above the shingle beach beneath the East Cliff; they date from the early eighteenth century, and were used as storage for fishing tackle and the drying of nets. They have been well restored and now form part of a Heritage Site; they appear in the oldest of town prints and, today, are the most popular subject for photographers!

SOME OTHER LANDING PLACES

A PASSAGE along the Kentish coast discloses few lengths of beach where there is not a boat of some sort drawn up, whether small fishing boat or dinghy; in every creek, whether attractive or not, there is almost always a mooring or two. In a sense therefore, virtually all the Cinque Ports and their Limbs which still have water, are capable of being explored from the water.

There are some that have enjoyed serious involvement with the Ports and retain a maritime interest, albeit now of predominantly local application. It would be a pity for the cruising sailor to remain unaware of their vestigial heritage, even if they are not to be included in an itinerary; given suitable conditions, anchoring off is an option for some.

Those who wish to explore the coast by dinghy will find useful, in addition to the usual requirements of a well-found craft, an outboard, inflatable beach rollers for launch and recovery, a decent anchor, and a hand-held GPS. There is a challenge, here.

The places described briefly in this section are included, therefore, on a combination of their having *some* facilities for the seafarer combined with a sufficiency of Cinque Ports' interest. Again, the descriptions follow the convention of an anti-clockwise order around the coast.

EASTBOURNE

Eastbourne was not a Member as such; it is credited with being represented at a special Guestling held at New Romney in 1596 to arrange for the provision of ships against the Dunkirkers, but there is no record of any positive outcome. The town is a substantial resort and the excellent modern Marina, about three miles to the east, is a good starting point for the 'Cinque Ports Itinerary' for those coming from the west. The marina is locked, and should be approached with caution in poor sea conditions; there is a very useful handbook available from the marina office.

i Cornfield Road   01323 411400
                               www.eastbourne.org
          Marina   01323 470099

HASTINGS

Hastings is always referred to as the Head Port, but perhaps because it is the first listed in accordance with the descriptive convention. This status was acknowledged at a meeting of the Brotherhood, although Dover was given precedence in matters of administration.

There are Roman traces, but it was the Jutes who were well settled there by the seventh century in the area adjoining the beach, although there is no remaining trace of this. The present-day 'old town' lies in the valley between the East and West Cliffs, linked by the promenade area to the more modern town to the west. In the valley run the courses of the Priory and Bourne streams, once exiting in the lea of the White Rock to form a useful harbour in Saxon times; the original port was a couple of miles further west at Bulverhythe.

The Saxon Chronicles describe Hastings as a place of importance. It was from the early times a substantial fishing port, and the men of Hastings were land owners on the east coast to facilitate their landing of catches and drying of nets, long before Yarmouth was established as a port in its own right; it is against this background that their deep-seated quarrels arose.

The town received its first charter from Edward the Confessor, and the Chronicles record that '... *the men of Hastings and thereabout fought two of Swein's ships and slew all the men and brought the ships to Sandwich to the king ...* '. The town's ship service at the time comprised twenty-one vessels, as for Dover, and more than the combined contributions of the fifteen vessels of Romney, Hythe and Sandwich. Their loyalty was short-lived because, when Godwin returned from France in revolt, they gave him full support; he was able to '... *entice to him all the Kentish men, and all the boatmen from Hastings ...*'.

At the time of the Conquest, both Hastings and Pevensey still possessed their mints. It is thought that William made a point of plundering the Hasting's Rape to force Harold into early battle but, for whatever reason, Hastings town was partly burned. It was soon rebuilt, but it was the 'new burgh' referred to in Domesday, although few lengths of the town walls are now traceable. It was William who was responsible for the reinforcement of the Saxon fort and, initially, he used timber prefabrications brought from France.

The increase in prosperity was due to its popularity for cross-channel passages; in 1093, Hastings Castle was occupied as a royal residence for about six months whilst William waited for fair winds for the crossing. The natural harbour was in the shelter in the east of White Rock, fed by the Priory stream, but it was never a large one; it was the port for the importation of stone from Caen used in the construction of Battle Abbey, and it became an important ship building centre in proximity to the vast forest of Anderida. At the time of King Henry I, in the early days of specialisation, it was responsible for both ships of war as well as merchant vessels, and also for Henry's '*Estnekta mea de Hastings*' - 'my Hastings yacht'.

In 1147, the Hastings fleet played a major part in the taking of Lisbon from the Moors, and it was in recognition of this that there is the curiosity of a priest of Hastings being installed as bishop there. The town was at the peak of its importance in the late eleventh and early twelfth centuries; it fell into decline because of the failure of its harbour following the rapid erosion of the exposed White Rock; in 1229, the Castle chapel fell into the sea and, in 1236, even the original St Clement's church had to be rebuilt on its present site. The onset of these reversals was the occasion of Seaford being granted to Hastings as a Limb and, in 1191, Rye and Winchelsea also. Subsequently, the town again proved fickle in its allegiance; in 1238, the French on their passage to occupy the Isle of Wight, having sacked Rye, landed at Hastings without resistance, and it fell out of royal favour as a result.

By 1544, it was so decayed that Seaford was granted its own charter, and it was not even mentioned in Raleigh's 'Discourse of Sea-Ports'. The ship service provided however, was distinguished and critical, and led to its being granted the Limbs of Bulverhythe, Petit Iham, Hidney, Pevensey, Bekesbourne [near Canterbury], and Grenche [or Grange, near Gillingham], but the non-corporate Limb of Seaford made little contribution; the Port survived into the sixteenth century, but it was regarded as impoverished. Queen Elizabeth I made grants towards the construction of a new harbour, but these were doomed to failure; the first attempt collapsed, and the second was thwarted by corruption; the last attempt at reconstruction of the harbour was in 1893, but the contractor was bankrupted and the site is now the seafront boating lake. The town only regained importance with the advent of sea bathing in the 1800's, followed by the development of St. Leonards.

Today, the old town is picturesque. There are the clapboard fishermen's net houses on the beach with the Fishermen's Church as an adjoining museum, and a small fishing fleet still launches off the beach with the tide; one curiosity is the tracked 'drots' used for hauling the vessels up the steep shingle. The main streets of High Street and All Saints' Street, following the original courses of the Priory and Bourne streams, retain numerous properties from the eighteenth century.

The Town Hall Museum displays a wealth of artefacts, including the coronation canopy carried by the Barons; this used to be presented before the shrine of St Richard of Chichester, in contrast to the eastern Ports who presented theirs at the shrine of St Thomas at Canterbury. Hastings Castle merits a visit, and it was from there that King John proclaimed England's 'Sovereignty of the Seas'.

Landing is on a steep-to shingle beach exposed to the south; the approach is on 000°T on 35°.700E, about midway between the two easternmost breakwaters, both of which should be given a clear berth at anything less than three-quarter tide. The facilities of the Hastings Motor Boat and Yacht Club include beach trailer-capstan and limited boat parking; there is a modern and hospitable clubhouse, but opening times are seasonal.

i Queen's Square   01424 781111

Hastings Motor Boat and   Yacht Club   -
                                          01424 429779

FOLKESTONE

Folkestone has a long history from 1052, when its ships were among those who supported the Earl Godwin. In the first half of the twelfth century it was joined to Dover as a non-corporate Limb and, from 1216, the harbour was the headquarters of King John's navy. In the 1278 charter of King Edward I it was referred to as 'Folston', but is recorded as having provided one ship only.

Its involvement with the ports was limited; it attracted a French attack only in 1339, when it was partly burned. Although the charter of King James I lists it as a Limb of Dover, there was a general decline in its importance from that time; The Black and White Books record that it was only in 1566 that it sent a representative to a General Guestling; further, in 1594, it was only paying a contribution of £1 against the Head Port's composition of £6.6s.4d.

The town expanded with the advent of Victorian holidays and the growth of cross-channel leisure traffic, but the modern quay outside the main harbour has been abandoned since commercial operations were transferred to Dover in 2001. There is little of present interest other than for the small colourful area adjoining the harbour.

Shoaling outcrops guard the entrance to this drying harbour, and formal pilotage notes should be studied. Within, the harbour is well sheltered; mud berthing alongside the wharf is not recommended because of the foul bottom and the poor ladder access; anchoring presents the difficulties of a multitude of small craft and unmarked ground tackle. Once ashore, there are no particular facilities for visiting yachtsmen.

BROADSTAIRS

Broadstairs was the port and ship building centre for St. Peter's, the most important of the villages that eventually were to become Margate, and as a non-corporate Member of Dover from 'time immemorial'. Many of the Margate *hoys* were built there and in 1565 it had eight boats and other vessels of two to twelve tons, manned by forty men. The chapel of St. Mary, in Albion Street, was once renowned for its image of our Lady of Broadstairs, to which passing vessels dipped their sails in salute; the statue has been removed to Canterbury cathedral. The tower of St. Peter's church was for a time used as a naval signaling station.

Broadstairs

The town has grown as a delightfully traditional family resort, with its sandy beach within a stone-walled harbour of an age similar to that of Margate, and managed by the Ramsgate Harbour Authority; it is a drying harbour, with dinghy sailing and a few other small craft. Entry for craft able to take to the sand is possible at the top of tide, but bathing activities make it unsuitable for substantial craft; there are no particular facilities for visiting yachtsmen, although there is a dinghy-sailing club.

Harbour Master   01843 861879

FORDWICH

Fordwich was the port for Canterbury, and where much of the stone for the building of the Cathedral was imported. The town was granted to the Abbey of St Augustine, Canterbury, by Edward the Confessor in 1055, and so remained until the dissolution of the monasteries. It was granted its own charter by King Henry I in 1111, under which it became a corporate member of Sandwich; it was granted another by King Henry II in around 1226, which is unique among the Cinque Ports in that it authorised a Merchant Guild, and at a time when it had temporarily severed its relations with the Ports. The Mayoral seal also is unique in showing a small fish in a basin, representing the importance of the town's trout fishery.

The village today retains a large handful of medieval properties and the Saxon church; the narrow bridge over the Stour provides a pretty scene. The old quays are still observable beneath the garden walling of the houses behind, and the Elizabethan town hall is attractive, overlooking the Town Quay with the gantry for the old 'ducking stool'; the Fordwich Boat Club is on the west bank, with its small river craft. There are the two excellent pubs that are very busy at summer weekends; of these, the George and Dragon is the older and better, but has no river frontage.

Fordwich

The passage up the River Stour from Sandwich takes about four or five hours by small boat, and is well worthwhile if there is the rare summer day when it is too hot to remain aboard or pass time in Sandwich. The use of the Town Quay presents no difficulties for dinghies or small motorboats, and the adjoining Fordwich Arms has a landing stage.

The river is tidal, with a range of about 0.15m at Fordwich; a minimum depth of about 0.6m is maintained except in conditions of severe drought. The air draft is restricted to about 2m at the Grove Ferry road bridge at the village of Upstreet where there is also a deservedly popular riverside pub.

MARGATE

Margate was not mentioned in the Domesday Book, but was geographically within the Hundred of St Mildred held by the Abbott at Canterbury. It is St John's village on the marshland behind Margate Bay that was a Member of Dover, and which has been absorbed by the town; its church of St. John the Baptist dates from 1124, and a St Ymar of Reculver is believed to be buried there.

In 1229 Margate was a substantial trading port and, together with others nearby, was ordered not to sell timber to the French. It was a disembarkation point following the Armada, and it was visited by Admiral Lord Howard who observed '*it is a most pitiful sight to see here at Margate how the men, having no place to receive them into here, die in the street ... it would grieve any man's heart to see them that have served so valiantly die so miserably*'; attempts at improvement met with the difficulty of conflicting authority between the Admiral of the Fleet and the Lord Warden.

The town grew from the servicing of merchant fleets lying in the roads awaiting favourable conditions to make the North Foreland, at which the first lighthouse was built in 1635. It boasted modest boat building and fishing industries and, at one time, there would have been over a thousand vessels lying in the roads; the piers have a history of their own, and the town Droits collection house still stands.

The harbour's inadequacies caused much of the shipping to have left by 1720, and it was regarded as insignificant until it expanded with the popularity of sea bathing. The town made many attempts to escape the administration of the Cinque Ports, but it only gained its corporate status in 1857. The harbour continued to attract a small commercial and leisure trade, and it was from here that Shackleton's *Endeavour* sailed for the Antarctic. It fell into an even steeper decline with the withdrawal of pleasure cruises in 1965, and the requirement for demolition of the leisure pier in 2000 brought it under the control of Ramsgate. The town's heritage mostly has been overlaid by modern development, but is discoverable with diligence.

The harbour has long been a drying one, severely exposed to the west. Anchoring on the sand within is unrestricted and a tender is superfluous at low water; berthing against the harbour wall leaves the risks of interference with the occasional fishing vessel, damage in heavy weather, and exposure to the raw sewage overlying the seaweed; daytime arrivals should report to the security officer, but berthing is free for an overnight stay. It is easy to be neaped there, and there are no particular facilities for the visiting yachtsman.

Margate - The Harbour and the *Droits* House

The best that can be said of a visit is that the receding tide rewards with a sight of the chronic silting that affected many of the Ports over the centuries.

i   The Parade   01834 583 334

GRANGE

Grange, earlier known as Grenche, lies on the eastern edge of Gillingham on the River Medway, and was connected with the Ports only because of the migration there of a family of Hastings, whose twelfth century feu duty was to provide one oar in the King's boat. The town of Gillingham applied for Cinque Port status on the strength of this connection, but it was refused as being insufficient

There are few traces of its past, although there is a nineteenth century history of local industry. The Cinque Ports public house is of no particular interest but, on the hill above, is a fine seventeenth century manor house that is now a residential home for the elderly. There is the very pleasant Riverside Country Park with decent facilities, and the informal riverside walk is in delightful contrast to the distant and industrialised north bank; there is a small creek nearby with private moorings, and leading to a concrete jetty with cleat and rings; there is a shallow slipway on the upstream side of the jetty, but there is a dangerous jumble of concrete blocks on the downstream side; there is a couple of hours' water there, just sufficient for a stroll and picnic.

To the east of the Park are a small promontory, Sharps Green's Bay of drying mudflats with occasional moorings, and something of a channel guarded by an abandoned barge. This unpromising course leads to the site of the old quay that survived into the twentieth century and is barely discernible by its remaining pile stumps; there is water there for perhaps an hour on the top of most tides. There is no serious recommendation to explore from the water, and the Medway Ports Authority would doubtless be pleased to receive mooring enquiries.

Grange - The Approach to Sharp's Green Bay

The interest lies in the circumstances of its association with the Ports. It is a salutary reminder that they were not simply all-powerful, but needed the economic support of numerous small communities to sustain both their arrogance and their service.

i   Riverside Park   01634 332706

Head of Jetty [GPS derived]   51°23.12N 000°35.95E

APPENDIX 1

SOME ALTERNATIVE TIDE-DEPENDENT ITINERARIES

General

THE ITINERARY requires particular attention to tides for access to some Ports and for cruising economy. There is little point in either trying to 'buck the tide' around North Foreland, or in allowing anxiety at the possibility of missing a 'tidal gate' at the destination, but some adverse tides are impossible to avoid.

There are the four broad alternatives offered, dependent upon whether a start is made from the south coast or east, and whether there is a morning or afternoon tide; this admittedly begs the question of just how early or late is 'morning' or 'afternoon', and all should be checked against a current almanac. It is worth considering the possibility of delivering the boat to, say, Eastbourne or Harwich a week or so beforehand.

The suggestions make some attempts to alternate between tidal mud berthing and marinas; they assume a cruising speed of 4kts. within daylight hours although, of course, there are opportunities to log some night passages.

The passages across the Thames estuary require specific recourse to formal pilotage instructions, and these are beyond the scope of this book; they are the most interesting, and provide great opportunities for practising dead reckoning! The routes suggested have merely been tried and found practical for a shoal-draught craft under the conditions at the time. In the event of bad visibility, the advice must be to stay put; if encountered on passage, particularly in the Thames estuary, the advice must be to find a suitable shallow and to sit it out having told Thames Coastguard of the situation.

STARTING from the WEST
Commencing at Eastbourne with a Morning Tide
Day 1: H.W-3. start for the 44nM to DOVER
It is best to start as early as possible!
Day 2: DOVER
Day 3: H.W.-3 start for the 15nM to RAMSGATE
This is about the easiest passage, and an opportunity to settle in.
Day 4: RAMSGATE
Day 5: H.W.-3 start for the 24nM to BRIGHTLINGSEA
A convenient passage is *via* the Edinburgh Channel, then cross-ing the Black Deep and the Sunken Sands at better than half-tide, followed by crossing the Barrow and Middle Deeps, before crossing the Buxey Sands at *Wallet Slipway* on the approach to the Colne estuary.
Day 6: BRIGHTLINGSEA
Day 7: L.W-1 start for the 38nM to FAVERSHAM
A convenient passage is *via* the *Wallet Slipway*, about halving the tide down the East and West Swin, before turning a little west of south on a course direct for the Swale.
Day 8: FAVERSHAM
Day 9: H.W. start for the 29nM again to Ramsgate
This entails catching the early morning tide.
Day 10: H.W.-2 start for the 6nM to SANDWICH
This may well entail an early start.
Day 11: SANDWICH
Day 12: H.W start for the 18nM to DOVER
This entails catching the morning tide
Day 13: L.W.-2 for the 30nM to RYE
Day.14: RYE
Day 15: H.W.-1 start for the 20nM to EASTBOURNE

STARTING from the WEST
Commencing at Eastbourne with an Afternoon Tide
Day 1: L.W. start for the 44nM to RAMSGATE
Day 2: L.W. start for the 29nM to FAVERSHAM
Day 3: FAVERSHAM
Day 4: H.W.-1 start for the 38nM to BRIGHTLINGSEA
        This entails an early start. A convenient passage from the eastern
        end of the Swale lies a little east of north, via *Middle Sand*,
        thence via East and West Swin, before crossing the Buxey Sands
        for *Wallet Slipway* and the Colne estuary.
Day 5: BRIGHTLINGSEA
Day 6: H.W.-4 start for the 24nM to RAMSGATE
        A convenient passage crosses the Buxey Sands at *Wallet Slipway*,
        and thence across the East Swin to leave *East Barrow* to the west,
        before crossing the Sunken Sand at *Sunk* whilst there is sufficient
        water. The passage is then *via* Fisherman's Gat and the North
        Foreland
Day 7: RAMSGATE
Day 8: H.W.-2 start for the 6nM to SANDWICH
Day 9: SANDWICH
Day 10: H.W -1 start for the 18nM to DOVER
Day 11: DOVER
Day 12: L.W.-1 for the 30nM to RYE
        It is better to leave earlier if possible.
Day 13: RYE
Day 14: H.W. start for the 22nM to EASTBOURNE

Note: *The difficulty with afternoon tides is making both Brightlingsea and Faversham, and hence the two days' passaging at the outset*

STARTING from the EAST
Commencing at Harwich with a Morning Tide
Day 1: L.W. start for the 41nM to RAMSGATE
              This entails an early start.
Day 2; RAMSGATE
Day 3: H.W-2 start for the 6nM to SANDWICH
Day 4: SANDWICH
Day 5: H.W start for the 45nM to RYE
Day 6: RYE
Day 7: H.W.-1 start for the 28nM to DOVER
Day 8: DOVER
Day 9: H.W.-3 start for the 15nM to RAMSGATE
Day 10: RAMSGATE
Day 11: L.W. start for the 29nM to FAVERSHAM
Day 12: FAVERSHAM
Day 13: H.W.-2 start for the 38nM to BRIGHTLINGSEA
              This entails an early start. A convenient passage from the eastern
              end of the Swale lies a little east of north, via *Middle Sand*,
              thence via East and West Swin, before crossing the Buxey Sands
              for *Wallet Slipway* and the Colne estuary.
Day 14: BRIGHTLINGSEA
Day 15: H.W.+5 start for HARWICH
*Note: The difficulty with morning tides is making both Sandwich and
Rye, and hence the two days' passaging at the outset*

STARTING from the EAST
Commencing at Harwich with an Afternoon Tide
Day 1: L.W. start for the 41nM to RAMSGATE
Day 2; RAMSGATE
Day 3: H.W-2 start for the 6nM to SANDWICH
Day 4: SANDWICH
Day 5: H.W start for the 45nM to RYE
Day 6: RYE
Day 7: H.W.-2 start for the 28nM to DOVER
Day 8: DOVER
Day 9: H.W.-3 start for the 15nM to RAMSGATE
Day 10: RAMSGATE
Day 11: L.W. start for the 29nM to FAVERSHAM
Day 12: FAVERSHAM
Day 13: H.W.-2 start for the 38nM to BRIGHTLINGSEA
        This entails an early start; the alternative is to anchor overnight in
        the Swale.
        A convenient passage from the eastern end of the Swale lies a
        little east of north, via *Middle Sand*, thence via East and West
        Swin, before crossing the Buxey Sands for *Wallet Slipway* and
        the Colne estuary.
Day 14: BRIGHTLINGSEA
Day 15: H.W.+5 start for HARWICH

Note: The difficulty with afternoon tides is making Faversham.

APPENDIX 2

DISTANCES

98	82	84	55	46	41	34	37	13	Harwich [*Guard*]
81	65	67	40	29	24	35	38		Brightlingsea
83	67	69	40	31	29	3			Faversham [Town Quay]
80	64	66	37	28	26				Faversham [*Spit*]
66	44	45	15	6					Ramsgate
69	45	47	18						Sandwich
44	28	30							Dover [Western Entrance]
22	2								Rye [Strand Quay]
20									Rye [Harbour]
									Eastbourne [Marina]

Approximate Distances in nM by the Shortest Navigable Route

TIDAL DIFFERENCES

HARBOUR		STANDARD PORT	DIFFERENCE on STANDARD PORT	DIFFERENCE on DOVER
Eastbourne		Shoreham	-0hrs15	-0hrs10
Rye Harbour		Dover	-0hrs20	-0hrs20
Folkestone		Dover	-0hrs10	-0hrs10
DOVER				
Sandwich	*Quay*	Dover	+1hrs00	+ 1hrs00
Ramsgate		Dover	+0hrs20	+ 0hrs20
Faversham	*Spit*	Sheerness	-0hrs15	+ 1hrs20
Faversham	*Quay*	Sheerness	-0hrs05	+ 1hrs30
Brightlingsea		Walton-on-the-Naze	+0hrs30	sometimes large
Harwich		Walton-on-the-Naze	-0hrs10	sometimes large

The tidal differences are approximations, and based on local observa-
tions; they are only for the purpose of preliminary passage planning.
There are ranges of differences; those between Brightlingsea/Harwich
and Dover are particularly large.
For Pegwell Bay [Sandwich], use Ramsgate.

BIBLIOGRAPHY – GENERAL

Bradley, A. G., 'An Old Gate of England' [1917] Robert Scott, London
Bradley, A. G., 'The Story of the Cinque Ports'
    [1925] D. Oliver, Broadstairs
Brentnall, M., 'The Cinque Ports and Romney Marsh'
    [1972] John Gifford Ltd., London
Boorman, H.R.P. 'Kent and the Cinque Ports' [1957] Kent Messenger
Brogger, A.W. and Shetling.H., [trans.John, K.],'The Viking Ship'
    [1951] Dryers Forlag, Oslo
Burrows, M., 'Cinque Ports' [1888] Longman, Green & Co., London
Garmonsway, G. N. [Trans.], 'The Anglo Saxon Chronicles'
    [1953] J. M. Dent and Sons Ltd., London
Green, I., 'The Book of the Cinque Ports'
    [1984] Barracuda Books Ltd., Buckingham, England
Harris, J., 'The History of Kent in Five Parts'
    [1719] Printed and sold by D. Midwinter, London
Hasted, E., 'History and Topographical Survey of the County of Kent'
    [1797-1801]
Hueffer, F. M., 'The Cinque Ports'
    [1900] William Blackwood and Sons, London and Edinburgh
Hugh, R., 'Fighting Ships' [1969] Michael Joseph, London
Jessup, F. W., 'A History of Kent'
    [1974] Phillimore & Co Ltd., London and Chichester
Jessup, R. and C., 'The Cinque Ports'
    [1952] Batesford Ltd., London and New York
Mais, S. P. B., 'The Land of the Cinque Ports'
    [1949] Christopher Johnson, London
Murray, K. M. E., 'The Constitutional History of the Cinque Ports'
    [1935] Manchester University Press, Manchester
Oliver, D. R., 'Late Medieval Thanet and the Cinque Ports'
    [1952] Batsford, London and New York
Page, W. [Ed], 'A History of the County of Kent'
    [1932] St Catherine's Press, London
Starkey, D. J. Reid, C., and Ashcroft, N., 'England's Sea Fisheries ...'
    [2000] Chatham Press, London
Villiers, A., 'Men, Ships and the Sea'
    [1973] National Geographic Society, Washington D.C.

BIBLIOGRAPHY - LOCAL

Brightlingsea
Benham, H. A., 'Essex Gold' [1993] Essex Record Office, Chelmsford
Dickin, E. P., 'A History of Brightlingsea' [1913] T W Barnes

Dover
Green, I., 'The Book of Dover' [1978] Barracuda Books, Chesham
James, J. B., 'Annals of Dover' [1938] Dover Express, Dover

Faversham
Percival, A., 'The Great Explosion at Faversham'
        [1985] Archaeologia Cantiana
Wilson, S., 'Faversham, the King's Port'
        [1963] Carmelite Press, Faversham

Hastings
Baines, J. M, 'Outline of Hastings History'
        [1989] Hastings Museum Publications, Hastings

Margate
Clarke, G. E., 'Historic Margate'
        [1967] Margate Public Libraries, Margate

Ramsgate
Benson, C., 'The Book of Ramsgate'
        [1985] Barracuda Books Ltd., Buckingham
Matkin, R. [Ed], 'The Ramsgate Fishing Industry'
        [1987] East Kent Maritime Trust, Ramsgate

Rye
Clark, C., 'Rye - A Short History' [1999] Rye Heritage Centre, Rye
Foster, J. and Clarke, K., 'Adam's Rye Guide'
        [1997] Adams of Rye Ltd, Rye

Sandwich
Bentwich, H.C., 'The History of Sandwich'
        [1971] Helen Bentwich, Sandwich
Gardiner, D., 'Historic Haven: The Story of Sandwich'
        [1954] Pilgrim Press Ltd., Derby

ABOUT the AUTHOR

Robert Crane was born in London in 1938. He was educated at the then Finchley Catholic Grammar School, failed miserably at Medical School, and then gained a degree in Estate Management.

He practised in Chichester as a Chartered Surveyor until his first retirement in 1988; he spent some years exploring Chichester Harbour and the Solent, until he turned eastwards and was lured by the Cinque Ports. He retired for the second time in 1998 and purchased his present boat, *Jemima Puddleduck*, a Peter Duck heavy displacement ketch-rigged motor-sailer.

After an extensive refit, she again became well known on the Suffolk and Essex coasts and thence into the Thames estuary, the Medway and the north Kent coast. *J.P.*, as she is affectionately referred to, is ideal for coastal exploration and enabled him to resume his interest in the Cinque Ports; this book is the result of his years of research and local knowledge.

He was married in 1968; he and his wife have two sons. His main interests, other than sailing, are parish work, Rotary and gardening.

The Author hopes that you have found this book
both enjoyable and useful.

Your constructive criticism for the next edition
will be welcomed.